Giant Fish and Happiness

by Captain Desmond O'Sullivan

For my Family and my Celtic Quest Family.
Thank you from the bottom of my heart.
We did this all together.

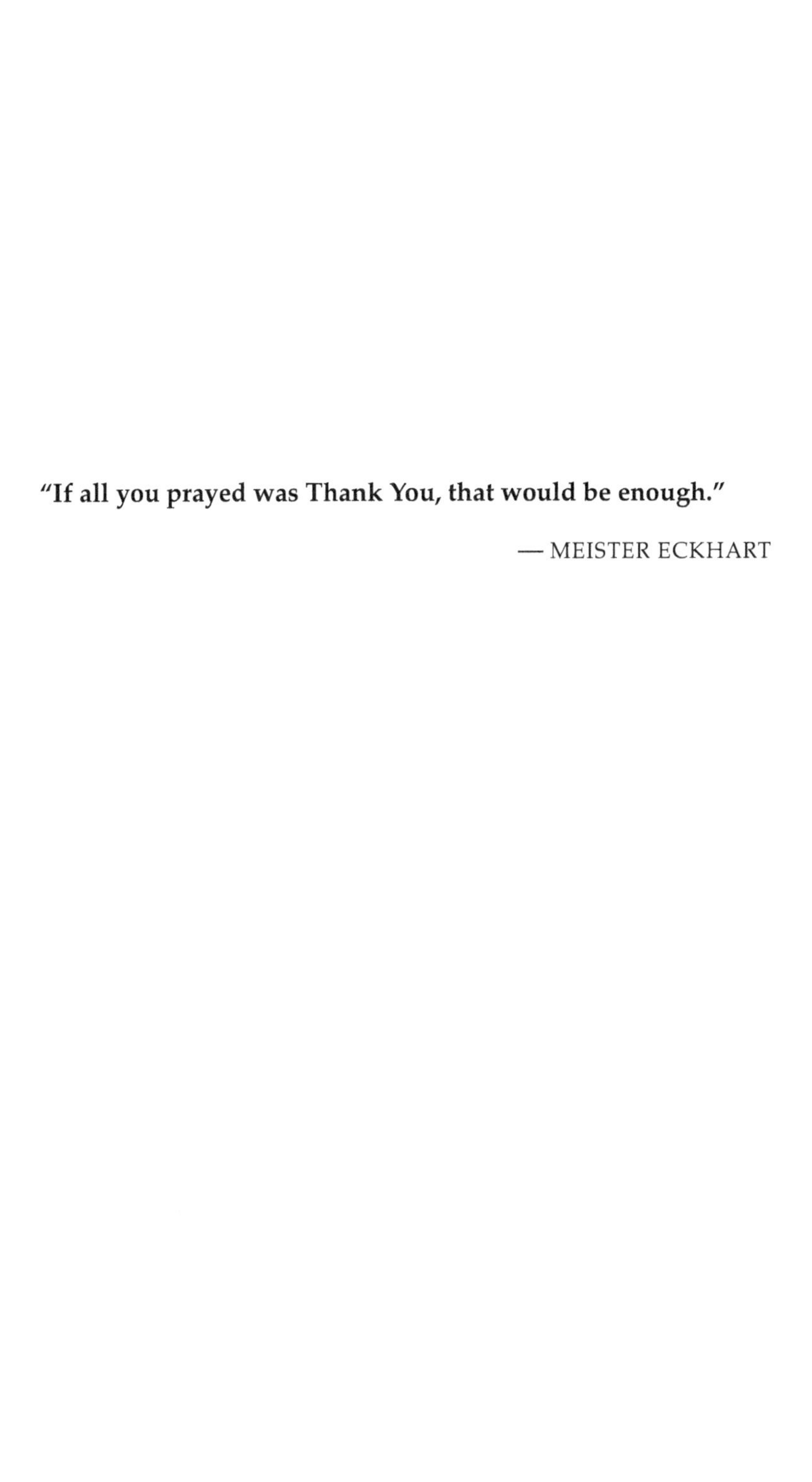

"If all you prayed was Thank You, that would be enough."

— MEISTER ECKHART

FOREWORD

Sometimes I wonder if my brother Desmond regrets the day I first invited him on to a fishing boat. I think about this every time he calls me when his engine has blown up and he has to cancel a week of full boats while it gets fixed. I think about this when he's in the shipyard in March and the temperature is below zero. I think about this when the fisheries regulators ignore what's in front of their eyes and restrict his ability to take his customers to where the fish are, or allow boats from a different state to fish right next to him but keep more fish of a smaller size because of where they are docked. I think about this every time the price of fuel and bait go up, or a crew member quits, or one of the other litany of challenges that any fishing boat captain faces.

But no, I know he doesn't regret falling in love with fishing. I know this because he sends me pictures of the sun rising over a placid Long Island Sound. I know this when he sends me pictures of a young kid who just caught his first fish and his smile is spread ear to ear. I know this when he sent pictures of our mom and dad sitting in the captain's chair or standing at the railing with their grandkids on a beautiful, sunny summer day.

This book is the story of the Celtic Quest fishing fleet, of a man and his love of the ocean, but it is a story of so much more. It is a story about the challenges and opportunities that come with building a business. It is a story about finding your soulmate and falling in love. It is a story about facing your own mortality and rising to the challenge. And it is a story about the love and support of your parents to help you realize a dream, and your love and support of them as their physical and cognitive abilities fade.

It is very interesting to read my brother's version of life, a life that I lived alongside him for so many years. His view of events that I participated in is especially fascinating. Reading a narrative of your own life as told by someone else was quite emotional, to say the least. Truly understanding his struggles with his own health and his relationship with our parents, as I lived 3,000 miles away, brought tears to my eyes chapter after chapter. Yet there is one story that my brother left out of this book that I wanted to tell because it has had an incredible impact on my life.

As you will read, in the spring of 2003, I had the privilege of coming to work on the first Celtic Quest for the spring blackfishing season. I was between jobs, moving from my coaching role at the University of Vermont to a new job in Michigan. Those five weeks I spent in Port Jefferson, living with my parents and my brother, family meals, heading to the boat every day that we could fish, and poring over maps of Long Island Sound at night to find potential new wrecks and fishing spots, is one of my fondest memories of home. We had so many incredible days on the water, and I had some of the best fishing days of my life.

That spring was a struggle for Captain Des, as each week he was not quite sure how he would pay the bills or whether the boat would hold up. He was always one engine breakdown away from catastrophe, and business was not exactly booming. One morning, we showed up to find five fares ready to go fishing, just enough to pay his fuel bill for the day. Yet there was a problem.

Two of the customers were already drunk and slurring their words at 6:00 a.m. I knew this would be a problem, but I told Captain Des not to worry about it. I could handle them, and he really needed their fare money to pay his bills. Then he said something that stopped me in my tracks.

"John, get those guys off my boat right now. I am building a business, and I want great customers. If that's the kind of customer I have to take out every day in order for this business to succeed, then I would rather that it fail."

I think about this story often, and I share it with many of my consulting clients who are building businesses and are unsure how to deal with disruptive customers. I share it because in that moment, I knew my brother had a crystal clear vision of the experience he wanted to provide for people, an experience similar to his childhood experience that helped him fall in love with fishing.

Over the past two decades, I have watched him build a flourishing business that is about so much more than catching fish. It is about providing people with lifelong memories of beautiful sunrises and sunsets, and of extraordinary days on the water with the people they love. Some of those days are marked by full buckets of fish, and others simply by time spent with great friends and family. And over those past two decades, I have never seen him waver from his philosophy that great customers would be the foundation of these great experiences and a great business.

I have also watched him bring this same love and compassion to our elderly parents, current and former employees, and valued friends and customers who are going through tough times. He has never wavered from doing the right thing instead of the easy thing, and he has never compromised on excellence in order to seek an easier path.

So, as you pick up this book and read the story of the Celtic Quest fishing fleet, the story of Captain Desmond's life, and the journey he has been on, not only on the water but off of it, I hope you will keep this lesson in mind. It doesn't matter what you do for a living. It matters who you are while you are doing it.

It was never about the giant fish.

It was always about the happiness.

John O'Sullivan

Bend, Oregon

PROLOGUE

THE SCHOOL BUS COULDN'T MOVE FAST ENOUGH. I SAT PRESSED AGAINST the window, watching the shoreline flash by and tracking the wind ripples across the water. Southwest. Perfect. The tide would be flooding into the bay right now, pushing baitfish tight against the beach. I'd been tracking the moon phase all week, circling today on my calendar. Everything lined up.

The bus finally squealed to a stop. I was out the door before it fully opened.

I hit our driveway at a full sprint, burst through the front door, and sent my school bag skidding across the floor. My rod was already rigged from the night before. I grabbed it and was back outside in seconds.

"Desmond? What on earth—"

I didn't stop. Couldn't stop. Through the yard, past Dad's vegetable garden where he was pulling weeds, down the path to the beach. Every second counted. The birds would be working already. The bass would be there.

Behind me, I heard the clank of his trowel hitting the ground.

"Come on, Dad!" I called back, not slowing down. "Perfect tide for the striped bass!"

In the distance, I could see them—gulls wheeling and diving, the water erupting in sudden swirls. The migration. Finally here.

"Yes! They're here!"

I was really running now. The bass were splashing in the eddy, maybe a hundred feet up the beach.

"Son, wait up!"

I turned. Dad was following, pulling off his work gloves as he hurried to catch up. He never followed me to the beach. He had his garden, his projects—always something that needed doing. But something in my voice, in my face, had made him drop everything.

"Dad! Dad, quick! You have to see this!"

I pointed toward the water where huge stripers were crashing on sand eels pinned against the shore, thirty feet out. The surface boiled with feeding fish.

"Look at all of them! I've never seen this many!"

Dad reached my side, breathing hard. His eyes went wide.

"Wow," he said. "What a sight, son." The excitement in his voice matched my own. "I've never seen so many striped bass in my life."

The biggest splash yet erupted right in front of us.

"Dad, I want you to catch one." I thrust the rod toward him. "Cast right there. Twenty feet."

"Me? Really?"

"Yes. Come on!"

He took the rod as if it were unfamiliar, turning it over in his hands. Then he pulled back and cast—a perfect arc, the lure splashing down exactly where I'd pointed.

"Great cast. Now just reel back. Nice and slow."

He started cranking. The lure wobbled through the feeding zone.

"There—get ready!"

A huge swirl engulfed the lure.

"Set the hook!"

Dad yanked back. The rod bent double. Line screamed off the reel.

"You got him! Just reel! Keep reeling!"

Dad leaned in, grinning wider than ever. The fish ran, then turned. Dad gained line. The bass jumped, silver in the evening light.

The fish tired, and Dad guided him into the shallows.

I waded in, grabbed the line, and slid the bass onto the beach. A beauty—thick shoulders, ten pounds.

Dad stared at the fish as if it were made of gold.

"I've never caught a striped bass before."

"She's beautiful. Let me get the hook."

I worked it free, cradled the fish, and waded back into the water. She was tired but strong. I rocked her gently in the current until she kicked.

"This is how you release them. Just like this."

One powerful thrust of her tail, and she was gone.

"Your turn, son."

I took the rod back and made the same cast. Three cranks of the handle and—*wham*—another one.

"You got him!"

Dad cheered as I released my fish. We took turns as the sun slid toward the bluffs behind us. Pure magic. Neither of us wanted it to end.

Then Mom's voice floated down from the house behind us.

"Boys! Dinner!"

Dad and I looked at each other, both a little disappointed.

"I guess we'd better head in," he said. "Don't want to get your mother mad at us."

We walked back together, his arm settling across my shoulders as we climbed the path.

"Son… thank you."

"For what?"

He smiled but didn't answer right away.

"Just thank you." He paused and then patted my shoulder. "One day you'll understand."

That evening—perfect tide, feeding bass, my father's arm around my shoulder, salt on his hands—something took root.

I said nothing. Sometimes, words aren't needed.

All I know is that in that moment, the compass of my heart swung toward its true north, and the call of the sea began to make itself known—quiet at first, but unmistakable.

PART I

THE CALL OF THE SEA

1

THE DAY EVERYTHING CHANGED

It's hard to believe that memories like catching striped bass with my Dad, or growing up on the shores of Mount Sinai Harbor, almost never came to be. Looking back, I realize just how easily it could have been different.

If not for Dad's hard journey before I was born, our family might not be here. Fate is fragile, and life's path often leads to unexpected places. My father's story became the foundation of my own journey toward the sea.

For my father, that path took a terrible turn one hot afternoon while working as a firefighter for the FDNY. It was there he found himself lying on a sidewalk in the Bronx, his back shattered, watching everything he thought he was supposed to be slip away.

My Dad loved being a New York City fireman. He lived it. He breathed it—just like his father before him. He wanted nothing more than to spend his life on the FDNY.

That plan changed in an instant.

A call came in. Apartment fire. A few blocks away. Dad and the crew grabbed their gear and jumped on the truck. When they pulled up, people on the sidewalk were screaming.

"Help! They're going to jump! Somebody help!"

Dad leapt from the truck before it fully stopped. His footing slipped, pain shot up his back, and he dropped his tools, collapsing on the sidewalk. The discs in his lower back—ruptured.

His world changed in a moment.

Three months in the hospital, weeks of rehab. He arrived angry, drowning in self-pity, questioning why he had to lose what he cherished most.

One day, the therapists brought him to the children's rehab wing.

There, he saw kids missing arms and legs, children in wheelchairs who would never walk again, and others facing illnesses far worse than his own.

"That's when I realized what sick people really look like," he told me later. "And I wasn't one of them. I stopped feeling sorry for myself."

Everything shifted.

The blow was tough, but he let go of the self-pity. He decided to focus on his blessings, not his losses. He worked his tail off in rehab. Got strong and even enrolled at Fordham University. Then he even went to law school, passed the bar exam, and started a second career.

One day, while picking a jury at court, he ran into an old college buddy who invited him to a Christmas party.

Dad showed up. Across the room stood a young woman—Kathleen Allen. Bright eyes. Beautiful smile. He fell in love on the spot.

As the story goes, that night, he dropped to one knee and sang to her in his tenor voice, *"I'll Take You Home Again, Kathleen."*

They fell fast in love and married within the year. They ended up having three children and a marriage of over 50 years devoted to one another.

Life took from him what he cherished most—his life as a New York City fireman. But it gave him something greater. His wife. His children. His whole family.

Amazing how it all works out.

2

A BEAUTIFUL LIFE

Mom and Dad settled into their home in Port Jefferson, a quaint historic village on the north shore of Long Island. Our house sat on the banks of Mount Sinai Harbor, where the sound of gentle waves and the ever-present smell of salt were a constant comfort.

Most days followed the same easy rhythm. We'd come home from school, drop our backpacks, grab our bikes, and disappear to find friends somewhere within a few square miles. We roamed freely, sun-kissed and barefoot, bikes tossed in piles wherever we landed.

The only rule Mom had was simple:

"Just make sure you're back for dinner."

More than anything, I loved the beach. Even at a young age, I knew the name of every little critter that lived along the shoreline. I could flip over a rock and tell you exactly what would scurry out from underneath it. I was endlessly fascinated by the sea—its rhythms, its secrets, and the way it always seemed alive. The beach was my sanctuary.

I felt closest to God there, long before I had words for what that truly meant.

But one activity stood above all the rest for my older brother John and me: fishing.

We were fanatical about it. It didn't matter what kind. If there was a line to cast and a chance at a fish, we were in. We'd fish from the shore, from docks, from anywhere we could reach the water.

"So," Dad would say with a grin, "who's the mightiest fisherman today?"

"I am! I am!" one of us would shout back, depending on who had the biggest catch that day.

Like most brothers, we loved the rivalry and the competition. But truth be told, neither of us really cared who caught more fish. What mattered was being out there together, sharing the same excitement, chasing the same dream—the Big One—just beyond the next cast.

Our first boat was a humble twelve-foot rowboat with a beat-up old six-horsepower outboard motor bolted to the back. She wasn't much to look at, but to us she might as well have been a yacht.

"Who gets to be the Captain today?"

"I am, of course," John usually answered, in true big brother fashion. Every now and then, he'd let me take the helm, but that was rare.

Those little adventures zipping around the local waters felt epic at the time—and in many ways, they were. Out there on the water, with nothing but a small engine and each other, we learned what it meant to trust. Not just the boat, or each other, but a trust that the world was somehow being guided by forces we couldn't see.

Those days were also quietly teaching us that timing matters. That delays aren't always accidents. And that what feels like misfortune can sometimes be a form of guidance.

Sometimes you don't recognize grace until you're standing in the place where it found you.

3

GOOD LUCK, BAD LUCK

"ALL RIGHT, WE JUST HAVE TO TAKE THE BOAT OVER TO THE FISHING Station for fuel, and then it's game on," my brother said.

We'd been having an incredible run of bluefish that week, and this was our last day before school started. The tide was perfect. The fish were waiting. We planned to make the most of it.

"You got the drain plug?" John asked.

"No," I said, confused. "I thought you had it."

"What do you mean you don't know where it is? We just got this boat. How the hell did you lose the drain plug?"

"You took it out! Not me!"

"You must have dropped it in the sand."

Typical teenage brothers—each of us certain the other was wrong. We kicked around the sand for a few minutes, but the plug was gone.

"This sucks," John said. "The tide's perfect right now. By the time we buy a new one, the bite will be over."

"Today was going to be the day, too."

We stood there for a moment, letting the disappointment settle. Then we turned and started walking back toward the house to see if Dad could drive us to the marine store.

We made it maybe twenty yards.

BABOOOOM.

The explosion hit like a shockwave. We spun around just in time to see a fireball erupt into the sky from the fuel dock, maybe a hundred yards from where we'd been standing. A forty-foot boat had blown itself to pieces. Through the smoke and flames, I saw the owner flying through the air like a rag doll. He landed in the water a good fifty feet from where his boat used to be.

"The fuel dock just exploded!" I was yelling it, but I could barely hear my own voice. "The fuel dock just exploded!"

People scattered from the marina in every direction. Somehow, the boat owner surfaced and began swimming. Another boater pulled him from the water.

John grabbed my arm. "Let's go. Let's go!"

We ran. We didn't know whether there would be another explosion, whether the fire would spread to the fuel tanks, or whether the whole marina would go up in flames. We just ran.

Then Dad came crashing through the woods toward us, moving faster than I'd ever seen him move. His face was white. His eyes were wild.

"You okay? You guys okay?"

"Yeah, Dad. We're okay."

He grabbed us both and pulled us into a hug right there in the woods, and I could feel him shaking.

"Holy crap," he said, his voice breaking. "I thought you were dead. You said you were going to get fuel. When I saw that explosion—"

He couldn't finish the sentence.

"We lost the drain plug," I said. "We couldn't go."

He pulled back and looked at us, and I watched it register on his face—the realization of what that lost plug meant.

"You lost the drain plug," he repeated, almost laughing. "Thank God. Thank God you lost the drain plug."

We walked back to the house together, the three of us, not saying much. Mom met us at the door, and the moment she saw our faces, she knew something had happened. Dad told her. She went pale, then pulled us in close.

I remember how good it felt to be there—hugging my mother,

standing in our kitchen, alive. All because we couldn't find a two-dollar piece of rubber in the sand.

What felt like frustration. What felt like bad luck. What felt like a ruined day may have saved our lives.

I didn't know the parable then. But I've spent a lifetime learning its truth:

Sometimes the thing you curse in the moment is the very thing that carries you safely home.

You just never know.

4

A WAY OF LIFE

"Come on, get out of bed, Des. You're coming with me. I need help on the boat today."

I felt the covers yank off my body.

"What? John, it's like five in the morning," I groaned, pulling the pillow over my head. "I just went to sleep."

"You've had plenty of sleep," he said, already halfway out the door. "Come on. I need an extra set of hands. You'll have fun---I promise."

"I'm not going."

There was a pause.

"Either you get out of that bed," he said evenly, "or I'm getting a bucket of water and pouring it on your head."

Older brothers have a way of winning arguments.

"All right. All right," I said, rolling out of bed.

John worked on a big party fishing boat---the kind that could carry sixty, sometimes eighty people at a time. Rods, reels, bait---all included in the fare. Fishermen came from all over the region to Port Jefferson just to spend a day on the water and bring home fish for their families.

The moment I stepped aboard, the smell hit me. Clams. Bait. Old fish racks still holding the memory of yesterday's catch.

When John said he needed "help," what he really meant was: *Come with your big brother, clean the buckets, and do all the dirty work while I make the money.*

That was fine with me.

He introduced me to the crew, and I took it all in. The deck was already filling with characters---blue-collar guys, factory workers, union men with calloused hands and weathered faces. They'd scraped together the extra money they had just to be there. Their voices were loud and unpolished, their jokes rough around the edges, but they were salt-of-the-earth in the truest sense. They loved fishing. Loved being together. Loved the escape.

Some had driven hours from the city, coolers in hand. All they wanted was a good bite and something fresh to put on the table back home.

John handed me a knife.

"Start cutting bait," he said with a grin. "And try not to lose any fingers."

I went right to work while he helped customers rig up and get settled. We steamed offshore a few miles, and then it happened.

Up ahead, acres of birds were crashing into the water as a massive school of bluefish surfaced to feed.

The Captain's voice boomed over the PA. "Get ready, everyone! There's a ton of fish right ahead!"

He maneuvered the boat closer, then backed down hard on the engines, stopping us right on top of the school.

Suddenly, the entire boat erupted.

Rods bent. Drags screamed. People yelled and laughed all at once. The crew hustled around the deck---gaffing fish, netting fish, untangling lines, doing whatever they could to keep up.

It was total mayhem.

Fish flying. Water spraying. Chaos everywhere.

By the end of the trip, every cooler on the boat was full---and then some.

As we tied up at the dock later that afternoon, exhausted and grinning, I finally asked my brother, "Hey... do you think I could come again tomorrow?"

John pretended to think it over.

"Hmm..." he said. "Yeah. Free labor? I think I can make that work. Be here at six. And don't make me drag you out of bed this time."

I continued on the boats with my big brother and within a few weeks, I landed a junior deckhand position of my own- and even started making a few dollars. I spent every possible moment on the boats after that, learning, eating, and breathing what it meant to be a fisherman.

I had no idea then that I was being quietly welcomed into a way of life---one that would guide me for decades to come.

It wasn't long before the boats became something of a family affair. John was already the senior deckhand, and I was working alongside him as a junior deckhand, learning the ropes. But one summer, we managed to convince the last person on earth you'd ever expect to join us---our sister Kait.

Kait is a beautiful soul, even then in her early teens. She had what I can only describe as fairy energy---creative, artistic, deeply sensitive---and she had gone vegan long before it was fashionable, long before any of her peers had even considered it. She wore rainbow hippie outfits and felt genuinely bad for animals. She was, in every possible way, the last person you'd picture standing on a fishing boat.

But somehow John and I talked her into it.

We put her to work running the galley, and before we left the dock that first afternoon, I brought her into the cabin and showed her what the job entailed. I pulled out the hot dogs and hamburgers and said, "Here---you'll be cooking these for everyone."

She looked down at them. Then she looked back up at me. Her eyebrows said everything her mouth didn't.

But she was in, and she knew it, so she rolled up her sleeves and got to work.

It happened to be an afternoon bluefish trip---notorious for attracting a raucous, beer-drinking crowd, and bluefish fishing is a bloody, chaotic business up on deck. At some point during the action, Kait poked her head outside to see what all the commotion was about. She took one look, shook her head as if to say, "Well, *this is certainly what I signed up for*," and headed back to her hot dogs without a word of complaint.

We also taught her how to tie rigs and lures for the customers, which turned out to be a real help. And despite all her moral misgivings about how fishermen love to live, she was a genuine sport about the whole thing---a hard worker who ended up being a terrific galley manager, hamburgers and all.

Those were good days. And with every trip, every tide, every fish brought to the rail, something in me was growing quieter and clearer at the same time. A dream began to form. Maybe someday, I thought, I could be a Captain too. Maybe I'd even have my own boat.

This dream felt invigorating, and the passion burned deep.

Some of my favorite memories from those years weren't just with my brother and sister — they were also with our Mom.

One winter trip stands out in particular. Bitter cold. Ice was forming along the rails. It was the middle of the night when she bundled us up in layers---hats, gloves, thick winter coats---herself included.

My Mom was a professional chef, and though she was exhausted from working nearly twenty hours straight the day before, she still drove us almost two hours to Montauk to catch a boat at the far end of Long Island.

As we climbed aboard the cold steel hull in the dark, the crew came around getting everyone ready. Mom smiled and waved them off.

"Oh no," she said. "Just my boys are fishing. I'm going to sit in the cabin and read a book."

Mom enjoyed the people aboard much more than the fishing. She struck up conversations instead — laughing, listening, sharing stories with whoever happened to sit nearby. She spent the day sipping coffee in the heated cabin while her boys stood at the rail, fishing through those frigid winter cod trips.

She worked so hard in those years. Sometimes I think she simply enjoyed slipping down into the bunk room and letting the rhythm of the waves rock her into a deep, well-earned nap.

It wasn't until much later that I learned something I hadn't known back then.

One night at the dinner table, years after those trips, my mother smiled and said, "You know, I actually didn't like fishing at all."

John and I were a little stunned.

"But nothing made me happier," she continued, "than seeing you boys out there with those big smiles on your faces, reeling in fish. Even when I was exhausted, those moments made it all worth it."

Only then did I understand what she had really given us- not just rides to the dock or warm meals afterward, but her quiet presence, her sacrifice, and her joy in watching us discover what we loved, as only a mother can.

Thankfully for her, John eventually got his driver's license and could take us fishing without dragging her along on our crazier adventures.

Not long after, John came to me one day and said, "Let's go on a three-day fishing trip."

We signed up for a special run that would steam nearly 120 miles offshore to the famous Georges Bank in search of cod. We'd read about those trips for years. Now it was finally our turn.

We were by far the youngest on the boat and mostly kept to ourselves---but we caught fish. Lots of fish. We filled every cooler to overflowing.

When we got back to the dock, we packed all those codfish into my family's old Plymouth Reliant station wagon, which my parents had loaned us. The weight was so heavy that the rear bumper scraped the ground on every bump.

Somehow, we got them home, sold the fish at the market, and even made back our fare.

We destroyed the shocks on my parents' car by hauling hundreds of pounds of fish in a little station wagon. They didn't get upset. As they saw it, the price of those shocks was worth every penny to see their boys so happy.

Those were among the most innocent and joyful times of my life.

Hard work. Simple moments. Shared laughter. Cold mornings and tired hands. It all felt perfect.

5

THE FIRST TIGHTENING

WHAT I COULDN'T SEE THEN---BUT CAN NOW --- WAS THAT WHILE THE SEA was quietly shaping me, another current was moving through my life at the very same time.

As much as fishing filled my days and my heart, there was something else that was always there too: soccer.

It had been part of our family for as long as I could remember, woven into long backyard battles with my brother and friends. I loved it. I was good at it. And for a while, the two worlds lived side by side without conflict.

But as I grew older, something began to change. Fishing remained a place of joy and peace, while soccer slowly became heavier. Expectations grew. Commitments multiplied. The path forward narrowed.

I didn't know it yet, but I was approaching the first moment in my life when I would be asked---quietly, but unmistakably---to choose what my heart was calling me to do.

Before soccer became something serious—before it became training schedules, travel weekends, and expectations—it was simply joy. We grew up with a soccer goal planted in the middle of our backyard, the grass worn thin and patchy from years of play. From the moment we could walk, my brother John and I were out there, taking turns pretending it was the World Cup final. We played until our legs gave out, until the light faded, until Mom called us in for dinner.

My Dad loved to garden, and his yard was filled with flowers—especially his prized rose bushes. Every so often, a shot would go astray and knock one out, or smash into the porch railings he seemed to be constantly repairing after another soccer ball found its mark. He would get mad at first, shaking his head at the damage. But it never lasted long. He loved watching us play too much. Before long, the anger would give way to a smile, and the game would continue.

When we weren't outside, we were in the basement. Dad cleared it out himself and lined the walls with plywood so we could practice for hours on end. That basement became our arena. We held epic skill contests down there—juggling battles that turned into family legend. Pencil marks showing who had the most juggles climbed higher and higher up the wall as all three of us—me, John, and Dad—traded places at the top of the leaderboard. It was always stiff competition, always close, and always filled with laughter.

Soccer wasn't just something we did. It was part of who we were. My Dad was a proud father, but he was also old school. Tough. He believed in discipline, in pushing hard, in earning success through effort and perseverance. He pushed us—not because he didn't love us, but because he did. Soccer mattered to him. Achievement mattered. Winning mattered. And as a young boy, there is nothing you want more than your father's approval.

When I succeeded in soccer—when I made a team, played well, pushed myself beyond what I thought I could handle—I could feel his pride. I heard it in his voice, saw it in the way he talked about me to others. That feeling was powerful. It felt good. It felt safe. On some level, chasing success in soccer became a way of earning that love and approval, even if I didn't fully understand it at the time.

Fishing didn't quite live in that same space for him. It was something I loved deeply, something that filled me up in a way nothing else did, but it didn't carry the same weight in his world. Not like soccer did.

When I was thirteen, a long-awaited phone call came in. "You're not going to believe this, but I just got a call from the coach! You made the

Olympic Development All-Star soccer team! Congrats, my boy! You did it!" I was thrilled. Proud. All those hours of training—staying late after practice, running on my own—it had paid off. But when I mentioned that I'd have to miss time working on the boats, something inside me tightened. I didn't have words for it yet. I just knew I felt it.

Training began almost immediately. Weeks of soccer camp. Endless drills. Long, punishing days under the summer sun. By the third straight week, my body was completely spent. I kicked off my cleats in the sweltering dorm—a brick-and-concrete box that trapped the heat like an oven—and sat on the windowsill, letting my feet rest for the first time all day. Outside, another team was running fitness drills in tight formation. I knew exactly how they felt—lungs burning, legs screaming, minds already dreading the next whistle.

Thinking about fishing brought me relief. I imagined the boats back home in Port Jefferson—the ones I loved working on, the ones that felt like home. I wondered what the wind and tide were doing, where they might be fishing at that exact moment. Just thinking about it made me smile. I really wish I were there. But alas, more training lay ahead.

6

MINNESOTA

THAT FEELING NEVER WENT AWAY. OVER THE NEXT SEVERAL YEARS, THE training only intensified. I moved up through the Olympic Development Program, and with each level, the demands grew heavier. We traveled to tournaments across the country and flew to Europe several times to compete against elite youth teams. The injuries came too—sprained ankles, tweaked knees, a couple of mild concussions that left me foggy for days. But we were good soldiers. We taped up and kept going.

One of the elite teams I trained with practiced all the way in Staten Island, more than two hours from home. Twice a week, plus games on weekends. My Dad would pick me up from school, and we'd fight our way through traffic on the Long Island Expressway as the sun dropped behind us. I'd sit in the front seat of his old sedan with my school books in my lap, trying to get my homework done before we arrived. Chemistry was the worst. I hated chemistry. Some nights, my eyes would start to close, my head dipping toward my chest, and Dad would reach over and tap me gently on the leg to wake me back up. After practice, we'd stop at Fiero's Pizza off Exit 63, or sometimes Carvel for milkshakes. It was our ritual—something small that made the long trip feel a little less like a grind.

Dad never complained about the drive. He believed in the work. He believed in me.

"Just hang in there," he said one night, pulling back onto the expressway. "You've got one more big tournament coming up. Minnesota. Then we'll get you some time off."

I nodded and leaned my head against the window, watching the taillights blur past. Minnesota. I could make it to Minnesota.

THE TOURNAMENT WAS one of the biggest we'd ever played in. Teams from across the country had come to showcase their talent. Our first game was a battle—still scoreless late in the first half when I saw a high cross sailing into our defensive zone. I tracked the ball, timed my jump, and felt my forehead meet it cleanly, snapping it back upfield. I was still in the air when everything changed. An opposing forward crashed into my legs. I flipped end over end and landed wrong, my arm collapsing beneath me as I hit the hard ground face-first.

When I finally looked down, I saw blood and my mangled arm. The game stopped. Trainers sprinted onto the field. Paramedics came next, splinting my arm and loading me into an ambulance. At the hospital, they rushed me into surgery to repair the compound fracture.

I woke up hours later in my hospital room, groggy and sore, my arm heavy in its cast. The window showed a sky I didn't recognize—flat and pale, nothing like the skies over Long Island. That summer had felt like it belonged to everyone but me. Between practices, expectations, and tournaments, I had been moving constantly—running hard, even when part of me wanted nothing more than to slow down and head back to the water.

But as I lay there, my mind began to wander. Visions of giant fish filled my imagination. I could almost feel the pull of a rod in my hands, the spray of salt water on my face, the rhythm of a boat rocking beneath me. Then my heart softened. I didn't have to struggle anymore. I didn't have to push through the exhaustion or pretend I wanted to be somewhere I didn't. My broken arm had given me permission to stop.

For the rest of the summer, I would just get to be a kid again. I would get to go fishing. And lying there in that hospital bed, far from home, I smiled.

7

BURNED OUT

Even with my arm in a cast, I could still be on the boat every day. That alone felt like a gift. I figured out how to prop the rod against my cast and reel with my good hand—and by the end of each trip, my pail was full. I kept fishing anyway, handing off the extras to passengers who hadn't had much luck. Every fish I gave away was met with gratitude, and somehow that felt just as good as catching them myself.

It was the best summer of my life.

When fall came, I returned to school and to the soccer field—both my school team and the Olympic Development Program. Just like that, the demanding schedule came rushing back. Weeks passed without a single chance to fish. Soccer had slowly turned into a full-time job, one I dragged myself to. As the weeks went on, I could feel the same familiar tension building in my chest, the same quiet resistance I'd felt before Minnesota.

I kept pushing anyway. I trained hard. I played well—despite the exhaustion. By the end of the season, I was voted Captain and MVP of my high school team. Scholarship offers from some of the top soccer programs in the country began arriving in the mail.

I should have felt proud. Grateful. Excited. Instead, I felt overwhelmed.

For several nights, I couldn't sleep. I lay in bed running the same questions in circles: How could I walk away from a scholarship? After everything I'd worked for? What would Dad think?

The acceptance deadline finally came. No more putting it off. That last night, I sat up in bed in the gray early light, looking at my walls. Soccer trophies on the shelf. Team photos. MVP plaques. A decade of work staring back at me. And next to all of it, in a simple frame my mother had picked out, was a photograph of me on the boat holding the biggest codfish I'd ever caught. I was wearing my grandpa's old flannel and holding the first fishing rod my parents had bought me for Christmas a few years earlier.

I looked at that picture for a long time. At the smile on my face. Not the tight, exhausted smile from the soccer photos.

"God, that was a good day," I said out loud.

When morning came, I sat there another minute, letting the feeling settle. Then I put my feet on the floor and took a breath.

"All right," I said. "I know what I have to do."

I got dressed and headed downstairs. Dad was reading the newspaper at the kitchen table when I came down.

"Dad, can I talk to you?"

"Sure, Des. Sit down." He looked at me over his mug. "You have a chance to think about those scholarship offers? Some really great opportunities there."

"Yeah. I've been thinking about it for weeks, actually."

"You should be proud. You busted your tail to get to this point. Having your college paid for—that's quite an achievement, son."

I didn't say anything. I stared at the table, afraid to meet his eyes.

"Son? You okay?"

"Dad, I'm not going to play in college."

He set his mug down. "You're kidding me. After everything you've been through?"

"I can't do it, Dad. I just can't."

"But why? I know you've been tired, but this is an opportunity most kids would kill for."

"I know." My voice started to shake. "That's what makes it so hard.

I'm burned out. I want to go to college like a regular kid. I just want to... be a kid again. I'm sorry."

For a moment, he didn't speak. Then he leaned forward and put his hand on my back.

"Son, please don't be sorry," he said, his voice softer now. "You don't have to apologize. I'm just surprised, that's all. You know I support you in whatever you want to do. You worked so hard to get here, and now you're walking away."

"I know it sounds crazy."

"I didn't say crazy. I'm just a little shocked, that's all." He paused. He gave my shoulder a squeeze. "If this is what you feel you need to do, then you follow your heart. That's all I've ever wanted for you."

"Thank you, Dad."

He nodded and picked up his mug again; something in his face softened. I think he understood more than he was saying.

I spent the next hour sorting through a stack of envelopes. One by one, I contacted the coaches and respectfully declined their offers. When I was done, I picked up the Fordham University application, where my big brother was also attending. I found the acceptance form and checked the box that said I would be attending. Just college.

I set down the pen and sat there for a minute, looking at the checked box. Outside the kitchen window, the morning had turned bright. I didn't know what was ahead, but I trusted the pull I was slowly learning to follow—the same one that had always led me back to the water and, somehow, to myself.

8

AN OPEN DOOR

"Come on, Des, let me show you around."

My brother John walked me across the quad, past the stone buildings and the old church tower, pointing out the dining hall, the library, and the fields where his team practiced. Going to school with my brother had been one of the deciding factors in coming to Fordham, and now here I was, trailing him through campus the way I had when we were kids exploring the docks back home.

John was a senior and Captain of the men's varsity soccer team. He introduced me to his friends and teammates, many of whom I'd competed against over the years in club tournaments and high school matches.

"Des, why the hell aren't you playing?" a few of them asked when they heard the news. "Come on, we could use a defender like you."

"Nah, I'm good, fellas," I said. "Taking a little hiatus to rest the old legs."

"Well, if you change your mind, let us know."

"Don't worry," I told them. "I'll be on the sidelines cheering for you."

John had already tried to convince me himself, but I had no desire to go back. The game had taken enough of my young life already, and I was ready to be a normal kid for once—no early-morning practices, no pressure from coaches, no weekends swallowed by tournaments. I wanted to enjoy myself.

And enjoy myself, I certainly did.

Like so many college freshmen let loose in New York City, I discovered that freedom without structure is dangerous. The bars in the Bronx that didn't check IDs too carefully, the house parties in off-campus apartments, the late nights that bled into early mornings. I'd stumble back to my dorm room as the sun came up, sleep through my alarm, and miss my morning class for the third time that week. Then I'd do it all again the next night.

By midterms, my grades had begun to suffer. By the end of the semester, I was failing almost everything. I remember sitting in my dorm room one afternoon, staring at a stack of unread textbooks, feeling the weight of all the classes I'd missed and all the assignments I hadn't turned in—and not caring enough to do anything about it. Something in me had come untethered, and I didn't know how to fix it.

John did his best to help me get my act together, but I just fell further behind. Finally, he reached out to his friend and mentor, Father McShane, the Dean of Fordham College, to see if he could do something.

Father McShane was a Jesuit with kind eyes and a gentle way about him, the sort of priest who made you feel like he had all the time in the world. He agreed to meet with me weekly, and I would sit in his wood-paneled office, surrounded by books and beautiful crosses while he tried to help me talk through whatever was going on inside me.

We met several times over the following weeks, but as time went on, it became clear he wasn't getting anywhere. I'd nod along and agree that I needed to change, then walk out of his office and do exactly what I'd been doing before. The partying continued, the classes continued to slide, and the confusion I felt about my life only deepened.

One afternoon, he leaned forward in his chair and looked at me with a directness I hadn't seen from him before.

"Des, you're a wonderful young man with a great heart," he said. "But I can see how lost you feel right now. In your own words, you're partying too much, you can't manage to drag yourself to class, and you have no idea what you want to do with your life."

"That's definitely true, Father," I said. "I'm feeling pretty lost."

"I know you are," he said gently. "And I believe you'll figure it out eventually." He paused, studying my face. "But I wonder if being in college is the best thing for you right now. Have you considered that?"

I sat back, surprised. This was the college dean telling me it was okay to leave.

"I'm very serious," he continued. "As much as I believe in the importance of education, college isn't for everyone—and it certainly isn't right for everyone at the same time. Sometimes the best thing a young person can do is step back, take a breath, and get some clarity before wasting more time and money on something they're not ready for."

I didn't know what to say.

"Have you thought about what you might do if you took some time off?" he asked.

"I've always wanted to travel," I said, and as the words came out, I felt something stir in my chest. "I've always wanted to see what life was like outside the country, to explore other places."

"Exactly," he said. "Sometimes venturing away from what we already know gives us the best perspective on our own lives. Where would you want to go?"

"My Mom's best friend from childhood lives in Kenya," I said. "She runs a farm out there with her husband and kids. She's invited me to come stay with them for years."

Father McShane smiled. "Africa. That's quite a place."

"The idea has always excited me," I said. "I just never thought I could actually do it."

"Well," he said, "why couldn't you?"

I waited for the catch.

"Des, I'm happy to let you take a leave of absence," he said. "Go see the world. Figure out what you want. And whenever you're ready to come back, the door will be open. No questions asked."

"You mean I can just come back?" I asked. "Anytime?"

"You have my word."

Something lifted off my shoulders—something I hadn't even realized I'd been carrying. "Thank you, Father," I said. "You have no idea what this means to me. And I promise, if I go, I'll send you a postcard."

He laughed softly. "I'll hold you to that. Best of luck to you, Des. I'll be praying for you."

I walked out of his office and down the hallway, and somewhere between his door and the stairs, I started to skip. I couldn't help it. The heaviness was gone, and in its place was something I hadn't felt in months—maybe longer.

The world had just opened up in front of me, and I was going to step into it.

It was time for an adventure.

PART II

DISCOVERING TRUE NORTH

9

PLAINS OF KENYA

WITHIN A FEW WEEKS, I HAD POSTPONED MY COURSEWORK, BOUGHT A plane ticket, and set out for the plains of Kenya.

The moment I stepped off the plane in Nairobi, the air felt different —warmer, thicker, alive. The airport buzzed with movement and sound: voices calling out, carts rattling across concrete, the low hum of organized chaos. I scanned the crowd until I spotted my Mom's friend waving above the sea of people.

"Welcome to Kenya, my boy!" she said, wrapping me in a hug that instantly made me feel at home. She grabbed my bags and steered me toward the car. "Ready for an African adventure?"

"More than ready," I said, grinning. "Thank you so much for this opportunity."

"It's our pleasure," she replied as we pulled away from the curb. "Your mother is one of the most precious people in my life. And it's wonderful to finally meet her son. Not to mention"—she laughed— "we can always use an extra set of hands on the farm."

"Well, I'm ready to work," I said. "I couldn't be happier to be here."

We merged onto the main road, and within minutes, the car jolted violently as we hit a massive pothole.

"Wow," I said, bracing myself. "This road is really beat up. Your poor car."

She laughed. "This? This is one of the good roads. You haven't seen anything yet. Wait until we get closer to home."

She slowed to a crawl, weaving around another crater in the pavement.

"You just learn to drive around them, Des. It's part of life here. We don't try to get anywhere fast—but don't worry. We always get there eventually."

She smiled as she said it, calm and unbothered, as if this were the most natural thing in the world.

"We've got a couple-hour drive over that mountain range you see ahead," she continued. "Sit back. Take it all in."

I pressed my face to the window as the landscape unfolded before me. Rolling hills stretched endlessly into the distance, layered in greens I didn't know existed. The land felt ancient, wide open, and impossibly alive.

"Oh my goodness—look!" I pointed. "Is that a buffalo?"

She glanced over casually. "Oh yes. They're everywhere. We have a whole herd that lives on our property."

"A whole herd?"

"Oh yes—and much more than that. Giraffe, hippos, impalas, lions, eagles. You're going to see things you didn't even know existed. It's like living inside a National Geographic movie."

As we descended the far side of the pass, the road turned to dust. We bounced along rutted paths until we reached a rusty gate, opened by a watchman who waved us through. A long driveway cut through fields of crops, leading toward a farmhouse tucked into the land.

"This place is incredible," I said quietly.

"It is," she agreed. "It's hard work. And Mother Nature isn't always the easiest partner. But we love it here. We love farming."

She pointed beyond the house. "On the other side are the grasslands that slope down to the lake. That area is teeming with wildlife."

"I can't wait to see it."

We pulled up to the house—a modest farmhouse surrounded by

chickens and roosters that scattered as we arrived. Suddenly, a massive Rottweiler burst through the door, charging straight toward me.

"Uh—should I be worried?" I asked.

"No, no," she laughed. "He's a big mush."

The dog proved her right, licking my hands and face enthusiastically.

"You're quite the friendly guy for such a big boy," I said, laughing.

Children's laughter drifted toward us.

"Kids," she called, "this is Kathy's son, Desmond!"

The two kids paused just long enough to size me up before nudging each other and sprinting off to continue their game.

"Come on," she said. "Let me show you around."

After meeting the rest of the family, she led me to my room.

"Here you are. This will be your home for now."

She gestured toward the window. "Take a look."

Beyond the glass, a herd of zebras grazed along the lakeshore.

"Zebras?" I said, stunned. "You have zebras here, too?"

"Plenty of them. Just sit and watch—you'll be amazed by what comes and goes."

I shook my head, smiling. "I can't even explain how happy I am to be here."

"Good," she said. "Wash up. Dinner will be ready soon."

That night, we shared a warm meal and easy conversation before the long journey finally caught up with me. I fell asleep almost instantly.

At dawn, the sound of roosters and unfamiliar birds pulled me from sleep. I stepped onto the veranda, blinking into the light.

The view took my breath away.

Lush plants and vibrant flowers stretched in every direction. The air was filled with birdsong, unlike anything I'd ever heard. High above, eagles circled effortlessly, riding invisible currents.

I grabbed a pair of binoculars.

"They weren't kidding," I murmured. "All of it really lives here."

For a long time, I just stood there watching.

My heart felt full—peaceful in a way I hadn't felt in years. For the first time in a long time, I felt like I was living according to my own heart, not someone else's expectations.

Over the next several months, I helped wherever I was needed on the farm. My Mom's friends were strong, gritty people—the kind you had to be to make a living farming in Kenya. They reminded me of the salty fishermen I'd grown up around: tough, capable, quietly generous.

On weekends, they packed up the family and headed out on camping trips to wildlife preserves that felt almost unreal. One afternoon, they invited me to join them on a trip to a remote island on a lake a few hours away.

"This place is very special," she said. "Quiet. Peaceful. Filled with wildlife. You're going to love it."

"You haven't disappointed yet," I said. "I'm in."

We left early the next morning, bumping along dusty roads until we reached the lake. Small skiffs were stacked along the shore.

"Grab your gear," she said. "We'll have the locals ferry us out."

As I approached the water, I froze.

"What… is that?" I asked, pointing to a pair of eyes gliding just above the surface.

"Oh, that's just a crocodile," she said calmly. "There are lots of them here."

"A crocodile?"

"Pay him no mind. Stay out of their way, and they'll usually leave you alone."

I wasn't convinced—but I stepped closer anyway.

"Don't worry," she added. "The locals know how to get us there safely. We've done this many times before."

Famous last words.

10

THE LONGEST NIGHT

"WHAT ARE YOU AFRAID OF, LITTLE CROC KID?"

The boatman grinned as he approached the skiff, his bare feet sinking into the muddy shore. "Come on, hop in. I'll make sure he doesn't hurt you."

He turned to my friends and winked. They all laughed.

"He's from New York," one of them explained. "Newcomer to these parts."

"Ah, I see," the boatman said. "I was wondering why he looked a little lost."

I stood at the water's edge, watching the crocodile slip beneath the surface, maybe thirty yards out. The water went still, which somehow made it worse.

"Don't worry, Des," my friend said. "You can trust him. He'll take us safely to the island. Hop in."

I threw my gear into the bow and sat down on the splintery wooden bench. The boatman pushed us off the beach with a long pole, and as we drifted out into the lake, he looked at me with something between amusement and genuine concern.

"You know, kid," he said, "it's not really the crocs you should be worried about anyway."

My ears perked up. "Oh, really? If not the crocodile, then what?"

"It's the hippos that will get you."

I turned to my friends, searching their faces for the joke. "Is that true, or are you guys messing with me?"

"No, it's true," the boatman continued. "Hippos kill more people than any other species in all of Kenya. You really have to stay out of their way. They hate people." He paused, letting the pole drip into the murky water. "I know you want to camp out here, but you'd better be careful."

"Great," I said. "I was just getting over the whole crocodile thing."

My friends smiled, but this time I wasn't laughing with them.

After a half-hour ride across the lake, we pulled our little boat onto the island's shore and unloaded our gear. We trudged through thick brush at the water's edge, branches scratching at our arms and legs, until the vegetation opened into a wide pasture maybe a hundred yards inland. Tall, golden grass swayed gently in the evening breeze.

"Up there, Des. That's a good place to pitch your tent."

"We'll be close by," another friend added. "Plenty of room. Go wherever you want."

I scouted the clearing and found a level spot near the highest point, where I could see the brush line in every direction. As I worked to set up camp, I couldn't shake the feeling that I had gotten myself into something I didn't fully understand. We had been safe on all our adventures so far, but something about this place felt different.

At nightfall, I made my way to my tent, unzipped the door, and crawled inside. The thin fabric walls glowed faintly from the last light in the sky. I zipped up the mosquito netting and lay my head down, trying not to think about what the boatman had said.

But his words kept circling back---hippos kill more people than any other species in Kenya.

"I pray to God they were exaggerating," I whispered.

Slowly, I drifted off to sleep.

I don't know how many hours passed before I woke.

My eyes shot open in the darkness. Something had pulled me out of sleep---a sound, deep and guttural, unlike anything I had ever heard before. A massive exhale, wet and low, vibrating through the night air.

I froze.

Then I heard it again, closer now. The ground seemed to tremble beneath me.

No. No way.

I lay perfectly still, my body rigid, adrenaline flooding my veins. The sound grew louder, each breath a slow, rhythmic bellows I could feel in my chest. I could smell him now---mud and rot and the thick, swampy musk of the lake.

It's a freakin' hippo!

My mind raced through options, but there were none. I couldn't run. I couldn't hide. The only thing between me and two tons of wild fury was a thin layer of nylon. All I could do was lie there and pray that this animal decided I wasn't worth killing.

The hippo moved closer. I could feel him now, the weight of his footsteps pressing into the earth just inches from my head. The fabric of my tent pushed inward slightly as he exhaled, his breath hot and damp against the side of my face. I held my own breath, afraid that even the smallest movement would provoke him.

The hippo took a huge bite out of the grass near my head.

He chewed slowly, rhythmically, the wet sounds of his massive jaws working through the vegetation. I lay there, suspended in a waking nightmare, waiting to see if the next moment would be my last.

He took another bite. And then another. I just lay there bracing for impact.

For the next three hours, the hippo grazed in slow circles around my tent, tearing grass from the ground with a sound like ripping cloth. I couldn't move. I could only lie there, trapped in a kind of purgatory, listening to the steady rhythm of his chewing and the deep, rattling exhale of his swampy lungs.

My whole life flashed before my eyes---not in some slow, cinematic way, but all at once, every moment compressed into a single overwhelming instant. I saw my mother's face. I saw my father standing on the dock back home, squinting into the sun. I saw my brother John laughing at something I'd said, my sister rolling her eyes at both of us.

I saw friends I hadn't thought about in years, and I felt the weight of every moment I had taken for granted.

Your mind does crazy things when you think you're going to die.

At some point, I just couldn’t take the torture. I reached slowly for my headphones and put on music to drown out the awful sounds. The music at least gave me something to hold onto, something to soften the terrible intimacy of his breathing while I waited to learn whether I would live or die.

Every few minutes, I lifted one earphone to see if he was still there. This went on for several hours.

Finally, around four in the morning, I heard the hippo moving away. His footsteps grew softer, receding toward the lake. Then came a massive splash as he leapt back into the water.

In that moment, I knew I had been spared.

I pushed myself up onto my hands and knees after hours of lying still. My muscles ached, and my whole body trembled as the fear I'd been holding back finally released. I took deep breaths, trying to steady myself.

"I'm alive," I whispered. "I'm still alive."

I started breaking down my tent as soon as there was a little light on the horizon, stuffing everything into my bag as fast as my shaking hands would allow, when I heard footsteps approaching through the grass.

My friends emerged from the gray light, easy and unhurried, letting me know the boats would be ready soon.

"You alright, Des?" one of them asked, watching me frantically roll up my sleeping mat.

I looked up at him and told him what had happened. He listened, nodded slowly, and then a quiet smile crossed his face.

"Yeah," he said, glancing at the others. "That happens sometimes out here."

They weren't cold about it---they were genuinely glad I was okay---but to people who had spent years living in this part of the world, a hippo grazing outside your tent was simply the bush doing what the bush does. They looked at this wide-eyed boy from New York with a kind of fond amusement, the way you might look at someone who had just discovered something you'd known your whole life.

I have never been so happy to leave a place as I was when we finally pushed off from that shore. I sat in the bow and watched the island shrink behind us, and I didn't look back.

I felt stripped down to something raw and fragile. Alive---but changed.

My thoughts drifted to my family. My Mom and Dad. My brother and sister. The same faces that had appeared so vividly in the darkness of that tent.

I had been completely alone that night---alone with my fear and my desperate hope to survive. And as the boat carried me back across the lake, I found myself asking a question I'd never really asked before:

If I had died out there, would I have had any regrets about how I lived?

In moments like that, the noise of life falls away. The things we spend so much energy chasing — status, money, approval — lose their weight. What remains is simple and unavoidable: how deeply we loved, and whether we had the courage to live the life that was actually ours.

These are hard lessons.

But unfortunately, some lessons don't come just once. They circle back, dressed differently, waiting to see if you've learned how to meet them.

11

TWICE SPARED

ONLY A FEW SHORT WEEKS AFTER MY ENCOUNTER WITH THE HIPPO, MY sister Kait came to visit me in East Africa. She, too, was filled with wanderlust and excited to join me on the adventure.

We made our way out to the coast of Tanzania, and soon it was time to fly back to Nairobi. Kait and I hopped on a flight out of Mombasa and found our seats by the wing. The plane took off, and we were happy, chatting away like we always did.

Fifteen minutes into the flight, out of the corner of my eye, I saw a massive flash. I turned, and all I saw was fire outside my window. The engine was fully engulfed in flames. The plane began to shake, then dropped rapidly from the sky. My stomach lifted into my throat.

People started screaming. Some cried. Some prayed out loud. Others just held each other.

"Calm down. It will be okay. Hang on."

The pilot's voice came through the intercom as the plane continued to drop, like being caught in extreme turbulence.

"Please, listen. We will be okay."

The Captain was trying desperately to steady the plane. A minute later, he came back on the intercom.

"The fire is isolated to one engine. We have cut the fuel and can fly on one engine. Please just hold on. We are returning to Mombasa for an emergency landing."

We were minutes from landing, but it felt like an eternity. I held my sister's hand as we tried our best to stay calm. The man next to us reached for his tray table, but he was shaking so badly he could barely secure it to the seat in front of him.

As we neared the airport, I looked out the window and watched through the smoke as the ground slowly moved closer. Everyone clung to their seats and braced for landing.

In those final feet, there was silence.

Closer.

Closer.

Then—impact.

The wheels slammed into the runway. The remaining engine roared in reverse as the brakes screamed beneath us. The plane hurtled forward, slowing, shuddering, until finally—mercifully—it stopped.

Emergency vehicles swarmed the aircraft, opened the doors, and began evacuating us. As we stepped onto the runway, everyone was in shock. Some cried. Others just hugged each other.

We made it. We were alive.

I looked back at the plane, smoke drifting into the air, and tears filled my eyes. For the second time in a few short weeks, I had escaped death—spared to live another day.

The memory of that night in the tent returned: the regret, the sorrow, the clarity that had shaken me. I had made a promise to myself then, though I hadn't yet known how to keep it.

Standing there on the tarmac, my legs still shaking, I understood something I hadn't before. Life wasn't just survival. It was an invitation. And whether I accepted it or wasted it was entirely up to me.

12

COMING HOME DIFFERENT

AFTER THREE SHORT MONTHS IN AFRICA, I RETURNED HOME. MY LIFE HAD changed forever.

The truth of how quickly everything can end—how close I had come to death—was no longer an abstract idea. It was etched into me. I had left for that trip a typical college kid, restless and distracted, moving through life on autopilot. I was coming home with something entirely different: a quiet gratitude for being alive and a humility I didn't know I was missing.

The moments with the hippo on that island and later with the plane had stripped everything else away. When you're forced to look directly at your own mortality, the world becomes astonishingly clear. All the noise falls silent.

I had been given a gift. I could feel it in my bones. And I knew—without hesitation—it was time to live differently.

It felt good to be back—really good. The comfort, the safety, the abundance of life in the United States struck me in a way it never had before. I hadn't realized how much I took for granted until I'd been stripped of everything familiar. I had gone halfway around the world looking for experience, adventure, meaning—and I came home carrying something much simpler: an understanding of how fragile all of this really is, and how careful I wanted to be with whatever precious life I had been given.

That summer, I worked full-time on the fishing boats—sunrise to sunset, salt on my skin, tired in the best possible way. With no distractions and no running from myself, something settled inside me. By the end of the summer, I felt ready to return to school—not out of obligation, but with intention.

Father McShane honored his word and allowed me to resume my coursework. This time, I showed up. I went to class. I studied. I cared. Much to my parents' relief—and my own surprise—I did well.

After a few months of steady, normal college life, another thought crept in.

Surprisingly, I was even ready to play soccer again.

The Fordham coach was someone I knew well from my days in the Olympic Development Program. He had offered me a spot once before—an offer I'd turned down. Still, I hoped. And I knocked on his office door.

"Yeah?"

"Coach—it's Des."

"Desmond!" he said, smiling. "How's retirement treating you?"

I laughed. "Actually... that's why I'm here. I think I'm ready to play again."

He leaned back, studying me. "You serious?"

"I am."

"Well, I'll be damned," he said. "We could really use you. You sure you're ready to play again?"

"I am, Coach. I definitely am."

"Well, if you can get yourself back in shape, pass the fitness test, and show me you still got it—the scholarship offer still stands."

I stared at him. "Really?"

"You play like you used to? Absolutely."

I thanked him at least three times before I left.

Outside, I couldn't help myself. "Yes," I said out loud. "I'm really doing this."

I trained relentlessly—early mornings, long runs, gym sessions, ball-skill drills every day. The time away had done what I didn't expect: it had given me back my love for the game. For the first time in years, soccer felt joyful again.

I passed preseason fitness tests and played well enough to earn my spot on the team. Fordham was a Division I program, packed with elite players. Balancing academics and travel was demanding, but this time I was different. I worked hard. I stayed focused.

By my senior year, we were one of the top teams in the conference. We won the Atlantic 10 Championship and advanced to the NCAA tournament, eventually falling to St. John's—the best team in the country. It was an incredible run, and I was grateful to be part of it.

I kept my grades up. I made up for the semester I'd taken off. I was even on course to graduate on time.

Not long ago, I'd been drifting—unfocused, careless with my opportunities.

Now, I was steady. Grounded. Present.

Amazing what a little perspective can do.

13

FOLLOW YOUR BLISS

THE COUNSELOR'S OFFICE SMELLED LIKE OLD BOOKS AND COFFEE. DIPLOMAS lined the walls in dark wooden frames, and a small window behind his desk looked out at nothing in particular. I knocked on the heavy door, and he waved me in.

"Good to see you, Desmond. Please, sit down."

I settled into the leather chair across from him as he shuffled some papers, then smiled.

"I've heard a lot about you. Even caught a few of your soccer games. Congratulations on the season—one of the best Fordham teams I've seen in all my years here."

"Thank you, sir. It was an honor to be part of it."

"So tell me," he said, leaning back. "Where do you see yourself going from here? You've got an excellent degree and good grades. The world is your oyster."

"Well, believe it or not," I said, "my greatest passion is fishing. I'd love to become a full-time fisherman."

He paused. His pen hovered over the legal pad.

"For real?"

"Yes, sir. Being on the water is what makes me happiest. I hope one day it can be my profession."

He tapped the pen against the desk, choosing his words carefully, then tilted his head to peer at me over his glasses.

"Des, that's great that you love fishing. But let's be honest here. There's really no future in it. It's too risky. Wouldn't it be better to use your degree? Get a real job—one with a pension and benefits?"

I didn't answer. I was getting the same message everywhere I turned. Even the captains I worked for and looked up to kept telling me how hard the business was, how poor the seasons had been, how I'd be a fool to pursue it. I was starting to believe them.

"You think so, sir?"

"I've been around a long time, Des. The kids who put their degrees to use, who get solid jobs—they're the ones who end up okay. Go get yourself something that pays well and offers some stability. You can always fish on the side, for fun."

"Yeah," I said quietly. "That's what everyone keeps saying."

"They're saying it for a reason." He set down the pen. "Tell you what—don't worry too much. We'll find you something good. Have you ever considered real estate?"

I hadn't. But before I knew it, he was dialing a friend, and I was walking out of his office with an interview scheduled for the following week.

The real estate company occupied an office with lots of cubicles and filing cabinets, and everyone was working away, papers strewn across their desks. Fluorescent lights hummed over rows of cubicles, and the air had that recycled quality of places where windows don't open. I showed up clean-shaven, hair combed, wearing the one suit I owned—feeling like a stranger in my own skin. For someone most comfortable in flannels and fishing gear, the collar felt like a punishment.

The interview went well. I got the job.

But within a few weeks, I was miserable.

The days passed slowly. I sat at my desk shuffling papers, watching the clock crawl toward five, my mind wandering to tides and tackle and the smell of salt air. The money was good, but I found myself staring out the window at nothing, just trying to get through the day.

One Friday afternoon, at 4:58, I was counting down the final minutes when my boss appeared at my door.

"Hey Des, I know you're about to leave, but I really need you to file these new accounts before you go. Any chance you could stay?"

"Sure," I said. "No problem."

I stayed two extra hours pushing paper while my fishing buddies sent photos from happy hour. One of them texted a selfie with a cold beer: *Hope you're having fun at your office job!* Lol.

Very funny, I wrote back. I sent him a picture of the pile of folders on my desk. *This is way more exciting. I know you're jealous.*

Des, your job sucks. You need a break.

They loved to tease me.

A few minutes later, another text came through: *What do you say we go to Montauk tomorrow? I hear they're biting good out east.*

I typed back immediately: *Now you're talking. See you in the am!*

We left at one in the morning, driving east through the darkness with the windows cracked and the radio low. Montauk sat at the very tip of Long Island, a small fishing village the locals liked to call "a quaint drinking village with a fishing problem." It was one of my favorite places on earth.

We arrived before dawn, the air still cool and sharp with salt. Boats rocked gently in their slips, and the sky was just beginning to lighten at the edges. We grabbed our gear and headed to the office to get our tickets, and that's when I overheard the Captain talking to his deckhand in the back.

"Man, this sucks. I can't believe we don't have any crew. What the hell are we going to do?"

"You got me, Cap. All I know is we need help—fast."

My friend elbowed me in the ribs. "You hear that? They need crew. You should apply."

"Nah," I said. "I just got a real job. I can't quit now."

"Des, what are you talking about? You hate that job. Nobody's making you stay there." He shook his head. "Screw it. I'm asking for you."

Before I could stop him, he walked right up to the Captain. "Hey Cap, I hear you're looking for crew. You should hire this guy." He pointed at me. "He's got a Captain's license and everything."

The Captain turned and looked me over. "That true? You got a license? You looking for work?"

"Well, I'm not sure. I kind of have a job already, but—"

"He sure is," my friend said, cutting me off.

The Captain nodded. "We start our offshore season soon. I'd be happy to give you a tryout. Here's my number. Think about it and call me tomorrow."

I stood there holding his card, a little stunned. My friend was grinning. "What an offer, Des. You've always wanted to work out here. You can thank me later."

We set out that morning into a calm sea under a brightening sky. The fishing was excellent—the kind of day that reminds you why you fell in love with fishing in the first place. Toward the end of the trip, I hooked into something heavy—a big codfish, maybe thirty pounds. I fought him to the surface, and the deckhand gaffed him, handing him over slick and beautiful in the afternoon light.

My friend called from across the deck. "You sure you want to keep that stupid office job, Des?"

I just laughed, holding the fish, feeling something I hadn't felt in months.

On the long drive home, my mind wouldn't stop racing. Every time I pictured my desk at the real estate office, a heaviness settled in my chest. But every time I thought about Montauk—the mornings on the water, the smell of bait and diesel, the weight of a fish on the line—something in me lifted.

By the time we got home, I'd made up my mind. The heck with the real job. The heck with what anyone thought. If I didn't give this a shot, I'd regret it for the rest of my life.

Monday morning, I walked into the office knowing I had to tell my boss. When I got to my desk, an email waited: *Des, when you get in, come by my office. There's something I have to tell you.*

I knocked on his door.

"Come in, come in." His face lit up. "Sit down, Des. I've got great news."

He leaned forward, genuinely pleased. "You've been working really hard. Doing a great job. And I'm promoting you to one of our senior sales positions. Not only that—I'm giving you a nice raise. Congratulations."

For a moment, I didn't know what to say. It was a good offer. A real opportunity. The kind of thing I was supposed to want.

But then I thought about the codfish. The weight of him in my hands. The way my friend had looked at me across the deck. The Captain's card was sitting in my wallet.

I took a breath.

"Thank you so much, sir. I'm truly honored. I didn't expect this." I paused. "But I'm afraid I'm going to have to decline. Actually, I'm going to resign. I'm becoming a full-time fisherman."

He sat up straight. "What?"

"I got offered a job on a boat in Montauk. I'm going to take it."

He stared at me for a long moment. "You're serious about this?"

"Yes, sir. I'm sorry. And thank you—really. I just need to follow my heart."

He thought about it a moment, then slowly stood and extended his hand. "Wow. Well, that wasn't exactly the answer I was expecting to hear. But, okay.... So be it." He stood up slowly.

"Best of luck to you, Des. I hope it works out."

"Thank you, sir."

We shook hands, and I finished up my work for a few hours, then walked out of his office for the last time.

That afternoon, I called the Viking Fleet in Montauk. "Cap—I'm in. I accept the job."

The next day, I packed a duffel bag with some clothes and my fishing gear, threw it in the back seat, and pointed my car east toward the end of the island. I blasted "Blue Sky" from the Allman Brothers with a big smile on my face. The windows were down, the late-afternoon light golden on the road ahead, and for the first time in a long time, I felt like I could breathe.

Montauk, here we come!

14

WELCOME TO MONTAUK

"ALL RIGHT KID. WELCOME TO MONTAUK. YOU READY TO WORK?" Captain Steve said as I walked up the dock with my duffel bag over my shoulder, the January wind cutting right through my jacket.

"I sure am, Cap."

Captain Steve Forsberg was the co-owner of the Viking Fishing Fleet with his father, Paul, both legends in our fishing world whom I had admired since I was a kid. Their family had pioneered new fishing grounds far beyond where most fishermen dared to venture, building their own fleet and pushing the limits of what was possible offshore. Steve carried that legacy forward, tough as nails but kind underneath it, the sort of man who would always treat you right if you worked hard. He had devoted his life to the water and to the company his family had built. I was excited to learn from him.

I hopped aboard and turned my face from the wind. The wheelhouse offered little more than a thin blanket and a space heater that looked like it had seen better days. It sputtered, sighed, and produced just enough warmth to remind me what heat used to feel like.

I added a few layers, climbed into the bunk, and lay there listening to the wind howl through the rigging. This was it. This was the life I had chosen. I pulled the blanket tighter and watched my breath hang in the air, and somewhere in that long, cold night, I must have slept, because the next thing I knew, gray light was coming through the frost on the glass.

I shook off the chill and added more clothes. The Captain and another deckhand were already boarding when I stepped out of the wheelhouse.

"Morning, Des. Ready to ship out?"

"Ready as I'm going to be, Cap."

"Hope that crappy space heater kept you warm and toasty last night."

I laughed. The last thing I wanted to do was complain, even though the truth was I had frozen my tail off.

"All right, let's go boys. Fire up the engines and let's head to the shipyard. About a four-hour steam."

We cast off the lines and headed for Rhode Island. Our vessel was a 140-foot steelhead boat, built to carry over 100 passengers at a time, with 70 bunks below for multi-day offshore trips. She was one of the most beautiful fishing vessels on the entire coast.

We arrived at the shipyard late that morning. A massive hydraulic lift was positioned over the water, ready to receive us. I had never seen anything like it---a machine capable of picking up steel boats, tugboats, and ferries as if they were toys.

"Don't worry, Des," Steve said, noticing my wide-eyed stare. "She'll pick us up like nothing."

The lift did exactly what the Captain promised. It picked our boat up like a feather and wheeled us across the yard, setting us down on land.

Steve grabbed his gear and turned to me. "Lots of work to do, boys. Time to get started." He gave me a look. "Des, lucky you. You get to hop down in the engine room and start cleaning up the bilge."

I pulled on my gloves and overalls. "Thanks, Cap. Couldn't ask for a better job."

He knew I was joking, and I knew the worst jobs always went to the new guy. That's how it works. Cleaning the bilge of a boat this size was not a quick task — I spent the next week chipping rust, scrubbing oil-soaked steel, and painting out compartments. The only hard part was that they had me working alongside another new hire who had just finished ten years in federal prison for assault. He was a real peach and spent most of his time complaining and goofing off whenever the Captain wasn't around.

Through it all, I kept my mouth shut and worked as hard as I could. The last thing I wanted was to come across as soft or lazy.

After a few hard weeks, we had the boat all cleaned up and ready to fish. We topped off the fuel tanks, pumped two tons of crushed ice into the fish holds, and stocked the galley with food. Finally, it was time for our first trip of the season.

We left Montauk around nine in the evening, and it was already blowing hard out of the southeast. Our destination was Nantucket Shoals, a prime fishing ground roughly a hundred and twenty miles from Montauk, southeast of Cape Cod. Captain Steve took us through Block Island Sound and past the northwestern end of Martha's Vineyard, but the coffee was wearing off, and eventually he let out a long yawn and turned to me.

"Hey kid, you ready for this? Your turn to drive. Your big moment is finally here."

"Absolutely, Cap. Go get some rest."

"Whatever you do, just be careful. This is your first time at the helm."

"I promise."

He stepped aside and disappeared into the bunk room. I put my hands on the wheel. I couldn't help but smile.

Over the next two hours, we passed the north side of Martha's Vineyard and Nantucket Island as we made our way toward the shoals. The wind had come up strong---close to thirty knots---and I knew that once we rounded Nantucket, we would be leaving protected waters behind and heading into the open ocean, where it would be much rougher.

As we cleared the Cape, I pointed the bow southeast toward the fishing grounds. The wind was howling through the antennas on the roof and rattling the wheelhouse windows. The swells were building, and soon we were launching off the face of one wave and slamming down into the trough of the next. A shudder ran through the whole boat each time we hit.

I kept the throttle where it was. The last thing I wanted was to slow down and have the crew think I wasn't tough enough or salty enough to run the boat. This was my chance to prove myself. So I pushed on, full steam ahead, pounding through wave after wave.

Then we launched off another big set, and another, and finally Steve came storming out of the bunk room.

"What the hell are you doing, kid? You have a death wish? Slow the goddamn boat down!"

I jumped up and grabbed the throttle, pulling us back to half speed.

"Cap, I'm sorry. I didn't realize---"

"Didn't realize? Kid, we're getting pounded out here. You've got customers below deck. Get your head out of your ass."

"Yes sir. I'm sorry. It won't happen again."

He turned and headed back to the bunk room without another word. I stood there at the helm, face hot, chest tight, definitely embarrassed. I had been trying so hard to make a good impression, and instead, I had shown just how green I really was.

I kept my hands on the wheel and carefully adjusted the throttle for the rest of the night, matching our speed to the seas, taking each swell as it came.

We arrived on the grounds at the crack of dawn. As the light came up, the Captain made his way out of the bunk room and stood beside me.

"Kid, what the hell were you smoking last night?"

"Cap, really. I'm sorry. I had no idea."

He looked out at the water for a moment. "Well, you've got a lot to learn. But for what it's worth, you did a good job the rest of the night. Those were hard conditions to navigate."

"Thank you, Cap. I appreciate that."

"Now suit up and go cut some bait. We're fishing within the half-hour."

I headed out of the wheelhouse and down to the deck. The rest of the crew was already gathered around the bait station, and one of them called out to me as I approached.

"If it isn't the seafaring cowboy himself. Morning, sunshine."

"Kid, that was some ride you took us on last night," another one said. "If I get tired early today, I'm definitely blaming you."

"I'm sorry, guys. It won't happen again."

"We're just messing with you. Stop with the long face."

The senior deckhand was standing off to the side, a cigarette hanging from his lip the way it always did, his leathery hands resting on the rail. His face was deeply lined and weathered, his voice like gravel, and he was the kind of man you would want beside you if things ever went sideways. He had seen more seasons on this water than I had been alive. As I walked past him, he put out a hand to stop me.

"Hey, Des. Pay them no mind. They're just giving you a hard time. We all have to learn."

He took a drag off his cigarette and looked at me with those pale, steady eyes. "There's a saying out here, kid. A good Captain knows when not to go. You understand what I'm saying?"

I nodded.

"Being sensible, being safe---that's what's going to keep you alive out here. Not toughness. Not pride. You remember that."

He held my gaze for another moment, gave me a nod, and then turned back toward the bait. "Now come on. Give us a hand with these skimmer clams. We've still got ten bushels to go before the first drop."

I picked up my clam knife and found a spot beside the pile. The shells had that faint, musty smell of the marsh, unmistakable if you've ever worked around them. The work was monotonous, but I had gotten fast at it over all those years on the party boats back home. The older guys noticed that I could keep pace. At least that was one less thing they could tease me about.

The shells clattered into the bucket one after another, a rhythm that asked nothing of me but to be present and to work. The sun climbed higher over the water, and I stayed at it, saying little, letting my hands do what they knew how to do best. Soon we would be fishing.

15

DAY IN THE LIFE

"Des. It's your turn. Come on, get up, kid."

I wasn't sure if I was dreaming. My body felt like a ton of lead, every muscle sore after thirty hours on deck.

"Really, Cap? It's been two hours already?" I struggled to open my eyes.

"Two and a half, actually. Gave you a little extra. I'm a generous man."

"Too kind." I swung my legs over the edge and sat there for a moment, trying to convince my boots to go on. "What's the big deal, right? Only another twenty-hour day ahead of us."

"There you go." He handed me a mug of coffee, steam rising off the surface. "Just remember—when your mind tells you it can't work anymore, you're only halfway there."

"Well, I definitely feel like I'm halfway there."

"Nah. You're just getting warmed up. Trust me, kid. There's always more in the tank than you think."

Coming from a man who'd worked these waters for forty years, I believed him.

I took the wheel, and he pointed to the GPS. "You see where we're headed? Western edge of George's Banks. Right where we left those fish biting good last trip."

"Got it."

"Watch the shipping channels. A lot of freighters out here. Wake us when we're half an hour out."

"Roger."

I decided to stand for the shift. Every time I sat, my eyes started closing on their own. The wheelhouse was musky and damp, the way it always was, smelling of cigarette butts and fish and something vaguely like diesel that never quite washed out. The instrument panel glowed a dim red so you could read it without losing your night vision, and I stood there in that faint light, hands warmed around my coffee, watching the radar sweep its slow circles.

The coffee was strong and acidic, the kind that had probably been sitting on the burner too long, but it was hot and caffeinated, and that was enough. It always hit the spot when you needed it to.

I took a long sip, and a sharp pain shot through my right hand and forearm. My fingers curled into a fist without my permission, the muscles seizing up hard.

"Son of a—" I shook my arm, trying to get the blood moving. The claw, fishermen call it. Days of gripping a fillet knife for hours on end, and your hands start to rebel, cramping uncontrollably. The skin on my palms was peeling from the salt water, crisscrossed with cuts I couldn't remember getting.

I worked my fingers open slowly, one by one, shaking off the cramps until I could grab the wheel again. Forty-nine nautical miles to go. A few large tankers showed on the radar, and I was grateful for them—something to focus on, something to keep me awake through the long dark hours.

In the wee hours of the morning, we finally pulled up on the grounds just as the sun broke the eastern horizon, painting the water gold. George's Banks spread out before us, teeming with life—birds wheeling overhead, the distant spouts of whales, and all along the horizon the shapes of other boats working the grounds. Trawlers and scallop boats dotted the water, always a welcome sight to know you had company so far offshore. A layer of fog hung low over the cool currents that ran through the deep channel east of the shoals, and you could feel the hard current pushing against the hull as we moved into position.

After fourteen hours of steaming, we'd made it.

"All right, fellas. We're here." I called into the bunk room. No one stirred. "Come on, it's morning. Time to work."

A few profanities floated back at me.

"Des, you just do everything today," someone grumbled. "We're staying here."

"Very funny. There's bacon in the galley. And coffee."

I think the mention of bacon did the trick as they slowly started stirring.

The Captain took the wheel, and I headed down to the deck. The customers were already lined up at the rail, eager, rods in hand. The Captain set the boat in the tide and keyed the PA. "Okay folks, let 'em go. Let's see what's biting."

The reels clicked into free spool, lines racing toward the bottom, and before I could finish my next sip of coffee, I heard it—"Fish on! Fish on! Two on! Four on!"

The whole rail was bent over with codfish. We grabbed gaffs and went to work, fish after fish coming over the rail for hours, a banner day unfolding under the morning sun.

After a few hours of great fishing, the Captain's voice came over the speaker. "Current's eased off and there's a ton of fish here. Let's anchor up. Crew to the bow."

"I got it," I called down to the other deckhands and headed forward.

THE ANCHORS SAT in the bow pulpit, huge hunks of steel attached to twenty-five feet of chain and a thousand feet of nylon line coiled on deck. Dropping them was always dangerous work, and you had to pay attention.

But when you're running on two and a half hours of sleep, your mind isn't as sharp as it needs to be. That's when things go wrong.

I looked up at the wheelhouse, and the Captain gave me the signal. I heaved the chain and anchor out of the mounting block, and with a heavy splash, the steel shot toward the bottom. The nylon rope started peeling off the deck at a vicious clip.

What I didn't notice was that I was standing in a loop of the line, something you should never do.

"Des, watch out!" One of the customers shouted.

Too late. The loop snapped tight around my right leg as the anchor screamed toward the bottom. I heard the line cinch down against the rubber of my boot, and then a massive force yanked me toward the bow, the pulpit rushing toward me fast.

I had maybe two seconds.

I grabbed for the rail, caught the last support rung before it ended, and held on. The rope cinched tighter around my ankle, pulling and pulling. Either the line lets go, or I let go. There was no stopping it.

Then, in one final agonizing moment, the line fired off my ankle—slid right off my wet foul weather gear—and my body dropped back to the deck.

I lay there, breathing hard, staring up at the sky.

"Holy crap, Des! You okay?" Faces appeared above me. "You okay, man?"

"Yeah. Yeah, I'm okay." My voice didn't sound like my own. "God, that was fast. That all happened so fast."

The senior deckhand—the same weathered old salt who had reassured me after my first night at the helm—knelt beside me and put a steady hand on my back.

"Never step in a loop," he said calmly. "And never let your guard down out here. The sea doesn't care how tired you are."

I nodded. I didn't need him to say more.

I stood at the rail for a minute, letting the adrenaline drain out of me. My heart was still pounding in my chest. I looked out at the horizon and let out a long breath, knowing how close I just came to serious injury or worse.

Then I shook my head, my hands still shaking as I put my gloves back on and went back to work. We still had a long, full day of fishing ahead.

16

WHALES

BETWEEN THE LACK OF SLEEP, THE LONG HOURS ON MY FEET, AND A NEAR-fatal accident the day before, I could feel it in every part of my body. I was shot, counting the minutes until the sun finally dipped below the horizon and signaled the end of the day's fishing.

Once in a while, to keep myself going, I repeated what the Captain had told me: *When your mind tells you you're done, you're only halfway there.* His mantra kept me moving, and somehow we made it to day's end. There were just a few more hours left at the fillet table, and we would finally be done.

Steve and I, another deckhand, hopped up on the cutting table on the stern and dug in. Steve was relatively new, like me, but a hard worker and a great deckhand. He was also the crew's comic relief, always cracking jokes, and everyone loved him for it. Tonight we worked mostly in silence, too tired for his usual humor.

As we neared the end, I gazed out at the night sky from time to time to distract myself while we worked through the final batches of fish. It was a serene, beautiful night on the sea, with a full, beaming moon rising over the horizon.

"Okay, Des—hard to believe this, but the last batch of cod is finally coming up," Steve said, dumping the final tote of fish onto the table with a tired smile. "Somehow we got it all done. Boy, that bunk is going to feel good after this."

"Sleep? What, are you tired or something?" I joked back.

Then we heard a strange sound coming from the side of the boat.

"Hey, you hear that?" I asked.

"Yeah, that was odd. Not sure what the heck that is."

At that point, I couldn't tell if I was just delirious. The sound came again—a murmur and a slapping on the water.

"It sounds like fins slapping the surface or something, right?"

"Yeah… like fins and—is that the murmur of a whale?"

"There it is again."

"Holy crap, that sounds like whales right next to the boat."

We dropped our fillet knives and ran to the rail to see what all the commotion was off our stern.

Six minke whales surfaced in the moonlight, all with their heads out of the water, bobbing up and down and looking back at us. Their skin was wet and gleaming, dark silhouettes against the silver light on the sea. They were just beyond arm's reach, close enough that I could have touched them with the end of a fishing rod.

There's no good way to explain what that feels like. Trying to describe it is like trying to explain love—you either know it or you don't. In that moment, time seemed to pause. We were two exhausted deckhands on a fishing boat, and they were ancient beings of the deep, gracing us with their presence.

"Holy crap, Des," Steve whispered. "This is unreal."

"I've never seen anything like this," I said, barely breathing.

For a long, quiet moment, we just stood there, locked in that exchange. It felt like a greeting. Or a salute. A wordless reassurance that everything—somehow—was exactly as it should be.

Then the largest whale lifted her flipper and slapped the surface once, sending a gentle ripple across the moonlit water. Slowly, deliberately, she turned and slipped back into the darkness. One by one, the others followed, their silhouettes dissolving into the night until the sea was still again.

Steve finally exhaled. "Did that really just happen?"

"That," I said, "was the most amazing thing I've ever seen."

We stood there a few seconds longer, neither of us ready to move, letting the silence settle back in. Then, without much said, we returned to the cutting table.

I picked up my fillet knife. My hands were sore. My legs felt like lead. I was utterly spent. But my body felt completely alive.

Most people would hear that description—no sleep, aching body, endless labor—and wonder how anyone could call it a good life. But moments like that—moments where you touch the mystery and wonder of the sea—change everything.

I could have chosen an easier path. Plenty of them. But I chose this one. And standing there under the moon, exhausted and grateful, I knew it in my bones.

There was nowhere else I wanted to be.

Not then.

Not ever.

17

RAINBOWS IN THE GALE

ONE TRIP LEFT IN OUR OFFSHORE SEASON. THE FORECAST CALLED FOR twenty to thirty knots---routine stuff we'd fished through a hundred times. But the North Atlantic doesn't care about forecasts.

Sixty miles offshore, steaming through the night, the cold breeze freshening from the southeast, the VHF radio crackled with an update.

"Gale Warning now posted. Northwest winds of thirty to forty knots are expected. Seas eight to ten feet."

"Where the hell did that come from?" Capt. Steve's hand stayed on the throttle, his thumb working the edge. "They said it was going to be okay."

"They keep upping the forecast every hour." I checked the barometer again, watching the needle sink. "We're going to get pounded, Cap."

"Damn. We're already this far off." He stared at the depth sounder, then the radar, his jaw working side to side — the tell that he was weighing risk against reward. Finally, he shook his head. "Screw it. It ain't worth it. We're headed inshore. We'll tuck behind Block Island and see if we can get the trip in there, sheltered from the wind."

We turned tail and ran back inshore for a few hours, anchoring near

Block Island as first light crept across the water. The crew and I prepped bait while the horizon slowly brightened.

The National Weather Service updated again. A powerful high-pressure system was racing down from the west to collide with low-pressure sitting offshore. The pressure gradient between the fronts was so extreme that thirty to forty knots wasn't even close to what was actually coming.

We fished for a few hours, keeping one eye on the horizon. To the west, a massive wall of clouds tumbled over itself as it approached. The wind had already climbed past thirty knots ahead of the front. Things were getting hairy.

"This looks nuts, whatever's coming," Steve said, lowering his binoculars. "This ain't going to be pretty."

He clicked on the PA. "Folks, please secure your gear. We're heading for home. It's going to get ugly fast once this front hits."

We hustled to the bow and hauled anchor as fast as we could.

"Everyone, remain in the cabin and hold on. We're about to enter some horrendous weather." The Captain's voice over the PA was calm, but his knuckles were white on the wheel. To get home, we had to steer straight into the front.

He turned to us, his crew. "All right, boys. This is going to be one hell of a ride. Engine room and compartment checks every fifteen minutes. Report back to me. And keep the customers inside."

"You got it, Cap."

We could see the front now — less than half a mile away.

Then it hit.

The wind slammed into us, shrieking through the antennas like metal tearing. The windows shuddered in their frames.

"Holy shit!" Steve glanced at the gauge. "Look at this---it's blowing over 70 knots!"

White froth tore from the wave crests, blown horizontal in a violent deluge of spray and vapor. We were barely making headway, pounding straight into the heart of the storm. In the cabin, the passengers sat silent. You could feel the fear.

Steve stood braced at the wheel, one hand clenched on the helm, the other riding the throttles, trying to time each wave. Despite his efforts, we kept going airborne — launching off steep walls of water, then slamming into the troughs. Each landing sent a shudder through the hull that you felt everywhere.

After an engine room check, I cinched my rain gear tight and headed back topside. The decks were awash, every step a calculated risk.

"Holy crap," I muttered, hauling myself hand over hand along the rail. The sea has a way of making you feel very small.

As we approached the shoals on the southwest corner of Block Island, the conditions worsened. Current ripped over the shallow bottom straight into the wind. Spray and vapor swallowed the boat until you could barely see. Subfreezing air pouring in from the northwest began icing everything over.

"We have to get over this shoal," Steve said, wiping condensation from the inside of the window. "My windows are icing up so bad I can't see a damn thing."

"I'm on it. I'll scrape the ice."

"Be careful out there, Des!"

I was halfway to the windshield when he pounded his fist on the glass and pointed. A towering wall of water was bearing down on us.

I crouched and braced.

We launched off the crest and slammed into the trough. The impact rattled my teeth, the vibration surging through my boots and up my spine.

"Goddamn, Cap! That was a big one!"

Your mind does strange things in moments like this. Fear spirals fast. What if we don't make it? What if the boat can't handle this? What if we have to abandon ship into that freezing sea?

This is what you dread as a fisherman. All those stories of boats lost and men who never came home---they live quietly in the back of your mind. You never really believe it can happen to you. Until suddenly, you're in it.

I did my best to keep those thoughts at bay. I could tell the rest of the crew and the passengers were doing the same.

Then I noticed another deckhand pointing over my shoulder.

"What?"

"Check out the rainbows!"

I shook my head. Had to be a joke. "This isn't the time, man."

But his arm stayed locked straight, his hand steady despite the pitching deck. "No, seriously. Look."

The entire sky was filled with rainbows. Not one or two — dozens, maybe hundreds. Huge arcs stretched across the horizon, smaller ones nested inside them, fragments and halos everywhere. Light poured through the torn spray and vapor, painting the storm in color.

We were trapped in the most terrifying moment of our lives, and at the same time, wrapped in one of the most beautiful sights I'd ever seen.

I stopped scraping ice. I just held the rail and stared. "Wow."

Another wave slammed us. The shudder ran up through my boots. Every fisherman-lost-at-sea story I'd ever heard flashed again through my mind.

Then something clicked.

We were either making it home, or we weren't. That part was already decided---by the sea, the boat, the Captain's skill, forces far beyond my control. Nothing I did in my head would change that. But I could choose what I focused on. The terror---or the rainbows.

I took a breath, steadied myself, and worked my way back toward the wheelhouse.

Hour after hour, we pounded over the shoal. Ice formed faster now, so we took turns scraping windshields just to keep visibility. No matter what happened, I returned to that thought: I can choose what I focus on. It became my anchor.

Eventually, we made headway into deeper water. And just as the sun dropped toward the horizon, Montauk Lighthouse emerged through the clouds.

As we slipped between the jetties and coasted down the face of one final wave, a collective exhale filled the wheelhouse.

"Holy crap. We made it." Steve stepped back from the wheel, his hands shaking. "Des, please dock this thing. I'm done."

"You did it, Cap," I said. "You got us home." He looked completely spent.

We tied up in our slip. Ice coated everything — the deck, the rails, the windows. Locals stood on the dock, calling up to us.

"I can't believe you guys were out there! We were so worried!"

"Yeah, that was a ride from hell."

More friends hurried down the ramp. "Thank God you're home!"

Most of the passengers couldn't get off fast enough. One guy actually bent down and kissed the ground.

We cleaned the boat and shut down the generators. The trip was finally over.

"Beers on me, boys," Steve said, his voice hoarse. "Time to celebrate that we're still alive."

Hell yeah.

The Dock---a salty bar where fishermen gathered---was just a few hundred yards from the marina. It smelled faintly of fish and diesel, but the beer was cold, and the company was good.

"Round of beers for everyone," Steve said as we walked in.

The bartender set them down. Steve raised his glass.

"I've been fishing for over forty years. I've seen weather you can't imagine. But that was the most horrendous ride I've ever had. Thank you all for the job you did. We made it, boys. We made it."

"Here's to you, Cap!"

Beer never tasted so good. A few more rounds followed.

That night, I went to bed dreaming of rainbows, grateful to be alive. I've never slept so well in all my life.

18

SOAKING WET

STORMS AREN'T THE ONLY THING YOU WORRY ABOUT AS A FISHERMAN. Mechanical breakdowns can be equally as scary.

One day, as we steamed north, I glanced down at my gauges and noticed the transmission pressure was way off. It was a beautiful day —flat calm, the sun pouring down—and I had eighty eager anglers on deck who had driven from all over the region to fill their coolers. The last thing I needed was mechanical trouble.

After anchoring on our first drop, I headed below to see what the issue was. I spent nearly half an hour in the engine room, toiling over the transmission in the heat, trying everything I knew. Nothing worked. I wiped the sweat from my brow and threw my wrench down onto the floor plates.

"Why the hell do you have to act up now, of all times?"

Maneuvering a hundred-and-forty-foot steel boat and producing fish for a crowd this size is hard enough with two engines. Now I had to do it with one. I took a deep breath and climbed back up to the wheelhouse.

"What happened, Cap?" my deckhand asked when he saw me. "Man, you've got oil all over you."

"The transmission's acting up again. I can't get it working."

"Again? I thought the mechanic just fixed that."

"So did I." I shook my head. "But whatever. I'm going to move the boat and set up on another drift over those fish, then come back down and give it another go."

"Figures on a day like this," he said. "Eighty people and the fishing's this good."

"Just keep an eye on the passengers and make sure they're having a good time. I'll let you know how I make out."

I maneuvered us back up the shoal on the one working engine and grabbed the mic. "Okay, folks, you can start fishing again."

The fish were on fire. Lines bent everywhere, and sea bass flew over the rails before I even had a chance to rig my own rod. I cast out and instantly hooked into a beautiful one, thick and dark with those striking blue markings.

"Now that's a nice fish," I said. "My favorite fish to eat."

"They're biting good, Cap. Real good."

"Well, at least we've got that going for us." I set my rod down. "That engine still needs tending to. I'm going to give it another go."

I was heading back toward the cabin when a passenger stopped me near the door.

"Hey Cap, what's going on with all this steam?"

"Steam? What are you talking about?"

He pointed toward the engine room. A wall of white vapor was starting to fill the cabin, billowing up from below.

A fire on a boat is a Captain's worst nightmare. I couldn't tell if it was steam or smoke, and all I could think about was what I'd do with eighty passengers if this boat caught fire. I was still a young Captain, and the weight of that responsibility hit me all at once.

I ran to the engine room door. Steam poured out around the frame and through the vents. I pressed my hand against the door—hot, but not burning. I pulled it open slowly, stepping back as the vapor rushed out in a thick white curtain.

"Please tell my crew to stand by," I said to the passenger. "I'm going in."

I pulled up my hood, held my breath, and started down the ladder. The rungs were slick with condensation, my hand sliding on the rail as the vapor made everything treacherous before I even reached the bottom. I dropped onto the floor plates, slippery with oil from the previous day's oil change and sharp with the smell of diesel from the fuel filters.

I stayed low, pressing myself against the greasy steel. Standing up was impossible—the heat was unbearable, and I couldn't see a thing. The big Caterpillar diesels clattered on either side of me, but even over their roar, I heard the violent sound of water blasting somewhere ahead.

I crawled toward it, pushing through a wall of spray and mist, until I found the source—the wash-down pump at the far end of the engine room. A fitting had blown clean off, and seawater was pouring in.

I fought my way through the deluge, water hammering my back and shoulders, until I reached the pump and slammed my hand against the shutoff switch. The torrent dropped to a stream, then a trickle, then a few final drops before it stopped. I closed the intake valve to make sure we couldn't take on any more water through that busted fitting.

The steam began to lift. I looked around at the damage. Every surface from the ceiling to the floor was dripping. The bilge had filled nearly to the floor plates, and those boards were just about to float. Another minute or two, and I don't know what would have happened.

I caught my breath and pushed the wet hair back from my face. If I'd managed to fix that transmission the first time, I never would have come back down here. I'd have been up in the wheelhouse, running the boat, with no idea the engine room was flooding beneath my feet. By the time I discovered it, we might have been in real trouble.

I climbed back up toward the cabin. Near the top, I saw a group of passengers gathered around the door, their faces tight with worry. Tom, one of our regulars, stood at the front. He looked at me like I'd just walked out of a wreck.

"Holy crap, Cap. You're soaked. What the hell happened down there?"

"Water leak," I said, still catching my breath. "It's fixed. We're safe."

I stepped into the cabin and dropped into a seat. My deckhand came over and handed me a towel without a word. He smiled and shook his head, knowing how close we'd come.

It's amazing how quickly things can turn—and how rarely you understand why in the moment. Something breaks. Plans unravel. You curse your luck.

And later, you realize it was the only reason everything else held together.

I folded the towel in my hands and wiped the water from my face.

I'd never been so grateful for a mechanical failure in my life.

19

TAKING THE PLUNGE

AT THIS POINT, I HAD SPENT SEVERAL YEARS RUNNING PAUL AND STEVE'S boats, and it was some of the best of my life. I was captaining vessels I had once only dreamed of working on, learning from men who had forgotten more about fishing than most captains would ever know. I should have been content. By any reasonable measure, this was a dream job.

But what happens when the dream that gets you here starts asking something more of you?

There was something in me that wouldn't settle—a restlessness that had been there since childhood, since the first time I held a rod in my hands. I had always known I wanted my own boat and business. In those months, that knowing shifted from a distant someday into something urgent and undeniable. I could feel it when I woke in the morning. I could feel it in my hands on the wheel. The call was getting louder, and I knew I couldn't ignore it much longer.

Somewhere between long seasons and epic fishing trips, I realized I was being asked to choose again—not between failure and success, but between comfort and calling. It was time to take the plunge. It was time to buy my own boat.

I woke that morning knowing a hard conversation lay ahead, but one I had to have.

I dressed and headed to the local deli. The smell of bacon and coffee drifted out the door as I opened it, a familiar comfort in a fisherman's early-morning routine. Fishermen lined up for egg sandwiches before heading out to work, and I stood there waiting for my breakfast, pretending this was just another day.

But it wasn't.

I had made up my mind. Now I had to say it out loud.

After breakfast, I walked the dock for a while, watching crews load bait and ice, telling myself I was waiting for the right moment. The truth was I was stalling, replaying the conversation in my head, asking myself the same question again and again. *Am I sure? Am I sure?*

The morning was crisp and clear. Gulls cried overhead. Water lapped against the hulls, and somewhere a diesel engine rumbled to life. I had walked this dock a thousand times. I had captained some of the finest boats on the coast from this very marina.

And now I was about to walk away from all of it.

Captain Paul, Steve's father and owner of the Viking Fleet office, sat dockside, close enough to the boats that he could keep an eye on everything. I stopped at the door, took a breath, and knocked.

"Come in."

He sat at his desk, nautical charts spread out in front of him, industry papers stacked to one side, a cup of coffee steaming near his elbow. He wore his white Captain's shirt with a few buttons undone at the top, and the weathered Captain's hat he was rarely seen without. Legend had it that the character of Quint from *Jaws* was modeled after one of the salty fishermen who had worked from this very dock—a man Paul had known well.

Paul easily could have been a character in that movie. He was just as legendary in the fishing community: a true pioneer, as salty as they came, honest and hardworking, a man who had built an incredible company and legacy with his own two hands. I had spent three years learning from him, and I respected him as much as anyone I had ever known.

Which made what I was about to say even harder.

"Capt, I need to talk to you about something."

He looked up from his charts. "What's on your mind, kid?"

I took a breath. "I'm leaving. I'm buying my own boat and starting my own fishing business."

Paul leaned back in his chair and crossed his arms. He didn't speak right away. He just looked at me, and the weight of his silence pressed down hard.

"What, are you out of your mind?" he finally said. "You want to do what?"

"I'm going to give it a try on my own."

"You know our industry is dying, right?" He shook his head slowly. "The regulations are killing us. Boats are going out of business left and right. The economy's in the tank. You really need to think about what you're saying here."

The words hit harder than I expected. This was the man who had taught me so much—not just about fishing, but about life and business. I had thought he, of all people, would understand.

"Des, listen," he said, his voice softer now but no less serious. "I'm all for people going out on their own. But I don't want to see you fail. This is not a good time to be doing this. You could lose everything. You understand that, right?"

"Yeah, Capt. I hear you."

And I did hear him. The doubts in my head grew louder. For a moment, I wondered if he was right. Maybe this was crazy. Maybe I should wait for a better time—a safer time.

But then something shifted.

"All I can tell you," I said, "is that I feel like I should do this. I've wanted it since I was a boy. Right or wrong, I feel like I have to give it a try."

"But why now?" Paul leaned forward. "Why right now, when so much is against you?"

"Why not now?" I heard myself say. "Why tomorrow? Why next week? Why next year?"

The words came faster, something rising in my chest. "My whole life, I've been told I'm stupid to want to be a fisherman. That I should get a real job, stop wasting my life, and put my education to work. That a life as a fisherman is hopeless."

I looked him in the eye. "And maybe they're right. But what if they're not?"

Paul said nothing. He just studied me, and something in his expression changed. Maybe he saw a little of himself in me—the young man who had once taken his own leap when everyone told him he was crazy.

He lifted his chin slightly.

"Kid, I think you're nuts," he said. "I think you're truly nuts."

He paused.

"But then again, I guess I was too, when I started this business. If this is what you want—if this is what you really want—then you have my blessing."

He leaned forward. "Just don't think for a second it's going to be easy. I busted my ass every day to build what you see here. I lost my shirt ten times over. Nothing comes easy. If you want to do the same, you'd better be prepared for what lies ahead. This is no small thing you're considering. And this is a really hard time in our industry to be starting from scratch."

He looked at me hard. "You hear me?"

I took a breath and let it out slowly. "I hear you, Capt. I wouldn't be doing this if I weren't ready. I'm all in."

Paul studied me for a long moment, then slowly extended his hand.

"Well then. Good luck, kid. I'm sorry to see you go. You worked hard for us. We'll miss you."

I took his hand and thanked him for all he had taught me, then turned and walked out of the office.

The sun hit my face as I stepped outside, and for a moment I just stood there, letting the morning settle around me. The Viking Fleet stretched along the dock—those big white-and-green steel super cruisers Paul had built himself. I had spent years aboard those boats, learning my craft, becoming the Captain I was.

And now I was leaving them behind.

There was fear in my chest—I won't pretend there wasn't. But there was something else too, a current running through me, bright and alive. I didn't know what was coming. I didn't know what I was walking into.

But I knew I had to find out.

PART III

LIVING THE DREAM

20

SAVED BY THE WIND

The diesel smell seeped up through the cold wood of the engine box as I lay there staring at the ceiling. Water stains spread across the white paint in patterns that told the story of years of neglect, and I made a mental note that this would need attention before the season began. I had just shut down the engine, and in the new silence I could hear water lapping against the old wooden hull—a soft, steady sound that seemed to say, *you're really here, you actually did this.*

I PUT MY HANDS BEHIND MY HEAD AND TOOK A BREATH. I HAD FINALLY bought my first boat, and she was all mine. I named her *Celtic Quest,* a nod to my Irish roots and to the feeling that this—whatever it was going to become—was something of a calling.

We were tied up at a fuel dock in New Jersey, halfway through a twenty-hour steam north to the shipyard on Long Island, where I would begin the long work of bringing her back to life. She had been built in 1957 by a well-known shipbuilder, and I imagined she was beautiful once. But after nearly five decades of service and a string of owners who had neglected her, she was well past her prime.

When I first stepped aboard to look her over, I noticed a spring in the deck that shouldn't have been there, and seam compound missing from between the old teak planking. The Captain's chair was worn through in several places, the white leather cracked and faded. The instrument panel was pitted from years of salt air. Down in the engine room, the old Detroit diesel looked like it hadn't been painted in a decade, and chasing oil leaks clearly hadn't been a priority for anyone in a long time.

I touched one of the wooden handrails and felt it wobble in my hand; the screws stripped out from the cap rail. *I'm going to have to fix that,* I told myself. It was the first of many times I would say those words.

But she was all I could afford, and I was so eager to start my own business that it may have blinded me. With rose-colored glasses firmly in place, I looked past the flaws and imagined full rails, bent rods, smiling faces, and long days on the water yet to come.

My friend Richie was kind enough to come along for the trip with me. He was a Captain out of Montauk with a generous soul and a lot of mechanical expertise, and I was grateful to have him along in case anything went wrong. He climbed down onto the deck with the supplies we needed for the rest of the trip.

"Boat's all fueled up, Des. Ready when you are."

I made my way to the wheelhouse, started the engine, and cast off the lines. As we broke the inlet and pointed the bow northeast, I tuned the VHF to the weather station to check conditions.

"For tonight, northwest winds increasing to twenty to twenty-five knots, seas four to seven feet."

"That wind's going to make it a long night," Richie said with a shrug. "It is what it is."

As darkness settled in and the temperature dropped into the high thirties, the seas built and began to test the old wooden hull. I could hear her creaking and groaning in ways that made me wonder if I had sunk every dollar I had into a vessel past the point of saving.

Richie heard it too. He was polite about it, careful not to offend me, but after we came off a few hard waves, he said, "Wow… she's a little creaky." Then he added, "We can put a few extra screws in her once we haul her out. Tighten her up a bit."

He was trying to reassure me. I could tell he had his doubts. I was having them too.

The lights of the shipyard finally appeared around three in the morning as we made our way through Fire Island Inlet and up the Great South Bay. We were exhausted, running on nothing but coffee and the promise of sleep. The entrance to the marina was narrow—a tight cut past an old wooden warehouse on the west side—and navigating it in the dark when you're bleary-eyed is not something I'd recommend. I slowed the boat to a crawl.

"We gonna make it through?" I called down to Richie.

"Yeah, you got it, Cap. Few feet on either side. Just keep her straight."

We eased through the cut and into the basin, tied off next to the warehouse, shut down the engine, and put the boat to bed after a long, cold night. I gave Richie a big thank you for helping me get through such a long trip with my new boat. We both packed up our gear and headed for home. I could barely keep my eyes open on the drive home to my parents' house. By four in the morning, I was through the door, up the stairs, and asleep before my boots hit the floor.

I woke a few hours later with one thought in my head: I couldn't wait to show my Dad the boat.

He was sitting at the kitchen table eating breakfast when I came downstairs.

"Morning, Dad. We made it. She's here, safe and sound. I can't wait for you to see her."

He smiled at my excitement. "Let's go check her out."

We grabbed a quick breakfast and drove toward the shipyard. I was telling him about the boat, about my plans for the season, about all of it, when I noticed his expression shift as we turned down the narrow street toward the marina.

"Son… what am I looking at here?"

I followed his gaze, and my stomach dropped. Where the old warehouse had stood just hours before, there was now a massive pile of smoldering wood and twisted metal, the street filled with smoke and the sharp smell of burned rubber and charred lumber hanging in the cold morning air.

"You've got to be kidding me."

The warehouse we had passed in the dark—just a few feet off our beam as we eased through the cut—had caught fire and burned to the ground. And my boat was tied up right next to it.

My father pulled the car up as close as he could. I didn't wait for him to stop. I jumped out and ran to the edge of the dock, my heart pounding, convinced that everything I had worked for was gone.

And then, through the smoke and steam, the silhouette of my little boat emerged. The white of her hull caught the morning light. She was still there. Still tied up right where we had left her. She hadn't burned. She was untouched.

I stood on the dock staring at her, not quite believing it. My father came up behind me, and I grabbed his arm and pointed.

"Dad, she's okay. The wind pushed the fire the other way. She's okay."

The same cold front we had cursed the night before—the one that brought the thirty-knot winds and made the trip so miserable—had saved her. If the wind had been blowing from any other direction, my boat would have been gone.

My father exhaled and closed his eyes for a moment, the way a man does when he realizes his son has been spared something painful. Then he looked at me and gave a small nod. No words. Just the quiet pride of a father watching his son have the courage to chase a dream.

I hopped onto the boat and extended my hand.

"Come on, Dad. Let me show you around."

And thanks to the wind from the night before, I helped him aboard for his first tour of the *Celtic Quest*.

21

50 SCREWS

THE SHIPYARD SAT ON WHAT USED TO BE AN OYSTER AND CLAM OPERATION, and a few times a year, they still dumped mounds of shells across the lot and crushed them flat with their machinery to keep the ground even. Cheaper than gravel, I suppose.

The faint smell of old brine hung in the air, mixing with the sharper bite of anti-fouling paint and polyester resin drifting over from the other boats hauled out around the yard. Sanders and grinders whined constantly, and the place was always full of fishermen and their hired hands doing the grunt work that keeps a boat alive.

"Dad, here's a box of fifty screws we can use to repair the deck. If you can just refasten the floor in the bow where some of the wood is coming up, that would be a huge help."

"You got it, son. Hand me the screw gun."

My father could see how much work I had ahead of me, and he jumped in like he always did. I think part of him worried I had bitten off more than I could chew. He got down on his hands and knees, bad back and all, and started working away.

It didn't take long.

"Des, is this all the screws you have?"

"Yeah, Dad. Why? Is that not enough?"

"Well, I've used them all up, and I haven't even made a dent. You'd better come see this."

I climbed down and knelt beside him. He pressed his hand into a section of the planking, and the wood crumbled beneath his fingers. It had been held together by nothing more than paint and habit, which probably should have been replaced years ago. My stomach tightened as I watched the soft, discolored grain fall apart in his palm. I couldn't help but wonder what other surprises were hiding in this boat, waiting for me down the line.

"You realize this is way worse than you thought, right?" he said.

"All right, Dad. No worries. I'll go get more screws."

I came back with 250. He blew through those, too, and still wasn't close to finished. He pointed to the entire area aft of where I was standing.

"That whole section is shot, son. Tons of rot. It all needs to come up."

I sighed for a moment, then regained my composure. "Well, it is what it is. Let's get to work."

We spent the next three weeks on our hands and knees together, fortifying floor joists, re-bolting timbers to frames, pulling out every piece of bad wood we could find. It seemed like every board we touched had another rotten one attached to it. I suppose that's what you get when you buy a boat that's been working the sea since the 1950s.

One afternoon, I was up on deck with my screw gun when I watched my Dad climb down the ladder—a rickety old aluminum thing, maybe fifteen feet tall, splattered with years of paint and fiberglass from being passed around the yard. He moved gingerly, one rung at a time, negotiating each step with his body. When he reached the bottom, he started limping across the crushed shell lot toward the shop, one hand pressed to his lower back, the other reaching down to help his right leg along.

One of the other boat owners looked over at me and hollered, "Man, what the hell did you do to your poor father?"

I laughed, but felt a pang of guilt watching him from above.

My father didn't turn around. He just gave a quick wave with the back of his hand and kept limping along. Tough old bird.

By the time we finished, we had gone through over one thousand screws, over forty bolts, and several boxes of nails—along with a few bloody knuckles, tired backs, and very sore knees. We had rebuilt the better part of the deck and finally got the old girl back into fighting shape.

"Dad, I can't thank you enough for sticking with me on this. I can't imagine having to do that by myself."

"Son, it's almost comical that you handed me fifty screws to start. That was a good trick."

I chuckled.

"You know, Des, I deserve a raise for this."

"You got it, Dad. Name your price."

"Well, right now you're paying me zero, so double it, and we're good."

He smiled and put his arm around me. My father had big, powerful arms, and his hands were nearly twice the size of mine. Meat claws, we used to call them. Feeling that arm around my shoulder reminded me of his strength—the kind he had done his best to pass on to me as a young man.

"I'm just kidding, son. I don't want any money. It's my pleasure to help you. What you can do is buy me a cup of coffee and a donut on the way home. We'll call it even."

"Deal."

After a few more weeks of work, the boat was shined up with a fresh coat of paint in Ireland's green, white, and gold colors. With Dad at my side and a heart full of excitement, the *Celtic Quest* was finally ready to head to her new home in Port Jefferson.

Now all that stood between Port Jefferson and us was a long run—over a hundred nautical miles—around Long Island, through New York Harbor, and up the Long Island Sound.

And one notorious stretch of water about to live up to its name, they called Hell Gate.

22

HELL GATE

WE CAST OFF FROM THE SHIPYARD AT THE CRACK OF DAWN AND MADE OUR way back down the bay and out through Fire Island Inlet. To get to Port Jefferson, which sits on the north shore of Long Island, we would need to go all the way around. The quickest route by far was to head toward New York City, up the East River, and then east down Long Island Sound. The entire trip would take about twelve hours.

As we approached the city, the skyline of Manhattan rose up in the distance. What a sight. Dad took pictures as I brought us into New York Harbor, and I could see him studying the water ahead, reading the traffic patterns the way he always did.

"Hey Dad, I don't want to steal all the fun. You want to steer for a bit and help me navigate through the city?"

"I would love that, son. If you want, I'll even take us up through Hell Gate."

"Man, you are a glutton for punishment, eh?" I teased.

"Ok kid, step aside. Let the veteran Captain take over."

Dad grabbed the wheel, and something shifted in him the moment his hands touched it. A kind of peace came over his face—a genuine glow I had seen so many times before. He must have been a mariner in a past life, because nothing seemed to make him happier than standing at the helm of a boat. He checked his bearings and began making his way up New York Harbor, present and alive in a way that only the water seemed to bring out in him.

It was a busy day in the city, with a huge amount of commercial traffic moving through—tugs and barges everywhere. We did our best to stay out of their way while keeping to safe water. Dad handled it all with his same steady calm.

"Ok Des, here's where it starts to get fun. Hell Gate, one mile ahead."

I could already see it taking shape—the channel narrowing into a series of S-curves beneath the bridges, the concrete walls on either side funneling the full force of the East River into that tight passage. The current ripped so hard through there that it created constant whirlpools, and I could see debris caught in them—branches and driftwood tumbling over themselves in the churning water.

"Wow, that current is already ripping hard against us. You weren't kidding. It's slowed us down almost six knots already!"

"Just wait. The worst part is right ahead."

"My goodness! There goes a huge branch of a tree, Dad! You see that?"

"Yeah, I see it. Altering course to port."

"Looks like there's even more debris coming at us. This place is like a minefield today."

"Don't worry. This ain't my first rodeo. We'll get through just fine."

A quarter mile to our north, I spotted a huge tugboat pushing a loaded barge downriver, coming right at us. The powerful current was on the tug's stern, accelerating his speed and dramatically cutting his ability to steer.

"You've got to be kidding me. Right when we're about to go through Hell Gate, this giant tug has to show up."

"Too late now, son. We're in it. We're just going to have to work our way around him the best we can. There's no place to really get out of his way in this narrow channel."

We battled against the current, lining ourselves up to pass as safely as possible. Then, out of nowhere, the engine started to sputter.

"Dad! Dad! Quick! Pull the throttle back! We're about to lose the engine!"

Dad grabbed the throttle arm and swiftly pulled it back to idle. The engine continued to sputter.

"We're going to lose her, Dad! Come on, engine! Don't fail us now!"

My heart was pounding out of my chest. If we lost that engine, there was no way we would avoid a catastrophic collision with the tug, now only a hundred yards off our bow.

Somewhere beneath the adrenaline, I heard my father's voice from all those years of fire stories at the kitchen table—stay calm, maintain composure, think clearly. When lives are in your hands, you don't get to panic.

I took a breath.

"Come on, engine. Come on," I said, talking to her, willing her to hold on. I could feel the hard current starting to grab our stern, trying to swing us sideways.

The engine sputtered one more time and then somehow steadied out at idle. I gave it just enough throttle to straighten the boat, but the moment I pushed it any higher, she tried to stall again.

We had no choice but to sit at bare idle, maintain steerage as best we could, and pray the engine held together long enough to pass the tug. I hailed him on the radio to alert him to our situation, but by the time he heard it, we were already too close.

I leaned hard to starboard. "Come on, engine! Stay with us!"

The bow of that barge—double the height of our boat—loomed over us, casting its shadow across the deck. The roar of the tug's diesels filled the air, growing louder as she closed in.

Then, in what felt like our last chance, the engine found its footing. With what little horsepower we had, we pulled just far enough clear to avoid collision. The massive barge thundered past, its wake rocking us hard as we clawed our way toward safe water ahead.

Dad and I turned and watched as the tug and barge passed us by, leaving a cloud of diesel exhaust hanging in the air.

"Holy sh—. That was way too close!"

"We made it, son. I think I might need to change my shorts after that one," Dad said.

"Figures—on a twelve-hour steam, the engine decides to break down in literally the worst two minutes possible."

"Ain't that just the way sometimes. Especially on the water."

"I think it's just a clogged fuel filter. That's why she's sputtering above idle. There's some safe water up here where we can pull over, and I'll change it."

We eased off to the side of the channel, and I climbed down to tend to the motor. It was a simple fix—just a clogged fuel filter, like I'd thought—but my hands were still shaking as I swapped it out. I took a few deep breaths down there in the engine compartment, letting the adrenaline drain away before wiping the diesel from my hands and heading back up to the wheelhouse.

Dad met me at the top, and for a few seconds we just looked at each other. Nothing needed to be said. We both knew exactly what the other was feeling—that deep relief of having just dodged disaster. Then a grin spread across his face.

"What the heck are you getting me into with this crazy boat of yours? You almost burned her down the first day you owned her, you handed me a box of fifty screws when we needed a thousand, and now you nearly get us killed by a giant tug and barge. What do you have planned next?"

"Hey, at least it's never dull with me, Dad. Right?"

"No. Dull, you are definitely not."

"All right, Dad. Enough excitement for one day. Let's get this little boat home."

Thankfully, the rest of the trip was uneventful. We steamed down the Sound with the wind at our back and the sun sinking toward the horizon, the air soft with salt and the occasional seagull gliding alongside us. I watched Dad at the helm, that peaceful glow still on his face, and let the hard days fall away—the purchase, the fire, the weeks in the shipyard, Hell Gate.

All of it is behind us now.

Father and son, heading home.

I didn't know what lay ahead, but in that moment, I felt peace—a quiet satisfaction that needed no words.

23

MUD BANK

After a short respite and a peaceful ride down the Sound, it wasn't long before life reminded us once again that this adventure, if nothing else, was not going to be dull. What we thought would be a routine check of the boat on her new mooring turned into one of the more comical moments to date.

THE SCREENS SHUDDERED AGAINST THE WINDOWS OF OUR HOME ON THE bluffs as the north wind picked up over Mt. Sinai Harbor. Dad and I were still a little tired from yesterday's trip through Hell Gate, but hopefully we had tied her up well enough on the mooring.

"Man, that wind is really going to pack a wallop later today, Dad."

"I thought you said it wasn't going to be that windy?"

"Well, compared to what's coming tonight, this is nothing. I think it would be a good idea to check the boat this morning and make sure everything is secure for the blow."

"I agree. Definitely wise. Let me finish my breakfast, and we'll take off."

We made our way around the harbor. The water was already white-capped as the north wind stiffened across the bay.

"Going to be interesting rowing out to the boat, son. You sure you're up for this?"

"We don't have much choice, Dad."

"I understand. Let's just hope it doesn't pick up any more."

We launched the **dinghy** off the beach just as a gust accelerated off the shore. The wind grabbed that light aluminum hull and pushed it like a toy.

"Weee!" I said. "Look how fast I can row, Dad!"

"Don't get cocky, kid. You still have to row back. Let's see how you do in the opposite direction."

"Ah, that'll be fun for sure."

We tied up alongside the boat and hopped aboard. Dad checked the lines and mooring while I inspected the compartments.

"Well, despite being tired last night, it looks like we did a good job. Boat looks A-OK."

A powerful gust blew my hat clean off my head.

"Yikes. Picked up even more just in the short time we've been on the boat."

"See, I told you. Don't get cocky. This is what happens."

"All right, for better or worse, let's try to get this dinghy back to the beach."

Dad pointed toward the shore, then swung his arm southeast. "Son, you realize the beach is that way—dead into the wind. If we don't make it, we're going the other direction, straight into the mudbanks."

"Trust me, I'm well aware. Either we make it to the beach, or it's mud central, here we come."

"Hop in first, Dad. I'll row."

I climbed in after him and took my first stroke. The wind hit me square in the face.

"My goodness, it's blowing hard."

"You got this, Des! Come on—what's a little thirty knots of wind in your face?"

I lay into the oars with everything I had, pushing with the full force of my legs.

We moved nowhere.

I pulled again. Still no forward progress. My forearms started to burn first, then the ache spread into my back. My lungs were on fire from breathing so hard.

"Come on, son. Got to really lay into those oars."

"What do you think I'm doing? I'm trying!"

"Kids these days. Can't you row any harder?"

"I know you think that's funny, but it really isn't helping right now!"

"Son, you've been rowing as hard as you can, and we haven't moved twenty feet!"

"Thank you, Captain Obvious!" I could barely get the words out.

The burning in my forearms and legs finally became too much. My muscles had nothing left.

"Dad, we're not making it. I'm toast. We're just going to have to let the wind take us and ditch the dinghy wherever we end up in the marsh."

"Come on! You're kidding me!"

"There's no way we're beating this. I give up. It's up to the wind now."

I stopped rowing and tried to catch my breath. The wind was already pushing us backward toward the wetlands, maybe a hundred yards off.

"Looks like we're going to end up on those muddy banks over there."

"Son, I'm going to kill you," Dad said, shaking his head—but laughing. "Really? This is how this is going to end?"

"Prepare for a crash landing on the swampy mudbanks, Dad."

We drifted with the hard wind until we hit the marsh with a thud. A blast of sulphur stench wafted over us the moment we landed.

"Oh, isn't this just lovely," Dad said.

"All right, Dad. Welcome to the mudbanks." I couldn't help but laugh, and neither could he.

"We're just going to have to carry this darn dinghy across the marsh and out to the road. Then I'll run back to the dock, grab my pickup, and come get you."

Dad took the absurdity in stride, the way he usually did.

"All right, let's do this. You grab the bow and lead the way."

"Oh, thanks, Dad. That way, if there are any sinkholes, I'll be sure to find them first."

"Well, you're the one who got us into this mess. It's all you, kid."

We were both laughing. What else could you do?

We picked up the dinghy and carefully made our way across the mud flats. My boots sank into the goo with each step, the mud making a loud sucking sound as it tightened around them, almost pulling them right off my feet. The sulphur stench was thick and putrid, and we did our best not to breathe too deeply.

"Hold on, son. I'm sinking. I'm sinking!"

I turned back. Dad had mud up to his knees. For a brief moment, his face flashed with genuine alarm—then, once he stopped sinking, the humor returned.

"Just hold the dinghy, and I'll pull you out!"

I gave a hard yank on the bow. There was a loud slurp as his legs released from the mud. He stumbled forward, caught his balance, and looked down at his boots, now coated in dark, goopy muck.

We slogged through the worst of it and finally reached the road. With our muddy legs on solid ground, we lifted the dinghy out of the reeds and onto the pavement.

"Well, that was fun, son. I've got to thank you for this. What a great day you've treated me to!" He grinned. "Now go get that darn truck of yours and get us out of here!"

At least we were still laughing.

I hustled back to the dock to get my pickup and drove back toward Dad, beeping the horn as I got close.

A fisherman stood near the road—scruffy, in a worn-out flannel, carrying a bucket and a folding chair, his rod tucked under his arm. He had clearly come to fish from shore. When he saw my father standing there, caked in mud, with a dinghy sitting on the side of the road, he looked utterly confused, like we had dropped out of a Twilight Zone episode. Then he started laughing.

"Hey buddy, what happened to you? Why are your legs covered in mud? And why the heck do you have a dinghy in the middle of the road?"

Dad shrugged. “If I told you, you wouldn’t believe how I got here. If you really want to know, you’d have to ask my son.”

We loaded the dinghy into the truck's bed.

“Wait till I tell your mother what you did to me today,” Dad said as he climbed in.

“Never a dull moment with you, son. That’s for sure.”

“Everyone needs a little adventure in their life, don’t they, Dad?”

“Well, you’ve been delivering plenty of that. And something tells me you’re just getting warmed up.”

Maybe he was right.

But standing there, covered in mud and laughing harder than I had in days, one thing was clear: sometimes, when life pushes you straight into the marsh, all you can do is laugh—and keep moving.

24

COLD START

The morning I had dreamed about my whole life arrived on a calm spring day with bright sunshine and barely a breath of wind. I drove around the harbor with my stomach full of butterflies, the kind that come from equal parts nervousness and joy. The *Celtic Quest* sat out on her mooring, freshly painted and ready, waiting for me to bring her in for our very first trip together.

FOR NOW, I HAD NO CHOICE BUT TO OPERATE FROM THE PUBLIC commercial fishing dock, since there were no berths available at the marina. The dock was home to countless commercial fish and lobster boats, many run by families who had worked these waters for generations. These were weathered men with calloused hands and sun-aged skin, hardened by life at sea, and they didn't take kindly to newcomers —especially some young kid launching a party-boat business from their dock. I did my best to keep to myself and stay out of their way, hoping that in time I might earn their acceptance.

One lobsterman in particular was an old German fellow named John who had been working out of this harbor for decades. Tough as nails, he barely offered a grunt for his morning hello, and most people gave him wide clearance as they passed. He was known as the guy you didn't want to mess with on the water, and people joked—only half-jokingly—that he might have a few unsolved homicides in his past. In the weeks prior, I had given him some extra bait I didn't need, which he accepted with a nod. So he at least tolerated my presence on the dock—for the time being.

"Morning, Captain Des!" I heard as I stepped out of my truck.

My old friend Capt. Neil gave me a wave from across the lot. "Reporting for duty, Capt Des."

Captain Neil was a retired Navy man I had worked deck for years earlier, back when I was just a kid. He was always dressed neatly and sharp, but beneath that crisp exterior was one of the warmest, kindest souls you'd ever meet. He was beloved in our industry—the kind of man who showed up for people without being asked. When he heard I was trying to get my business off the ground, he offered to help me on opening day. That was just who he was.

"Neil, I truly appreciate you coming out," I said.

"Des, you and I spent many good days on the water together. You worked hard for me back then. It's the least I can do."

"Well then," I said, "let's get this party started. Just need to hop in the dinghy and get the boat off the mooring."

We picked up the little rowboat and walked it down to the water. I climbed in first and grabbed the oars while Neil pushed us off the beach and settled into the stern. A few of my first customers had already gathered near the dock, waiting. I could feel John the lobsterman and the other fisherman watching from the corners of their eyes as they loaded their gear, curious whether this punk kid was for real or not.

Neil gave us a good shove, and we drifted off the beach into deeper water on that cold spring morning, both of us bundled in hooded sweatshirts and foul-weather gear.

"Here we go, Des!" Neil said with a grin.

Then I saw it.

The oarlock on the starboard side hadn't been secured. One of the oars popped loose and began floating away from us, drifting just out of reach.

"I'll get it!" Neil said, lunging toward the oar.

"No, Neil—don't lean over that far!"

But it was too late. In his earnest attempt to retrieve the oar, Neil's weight drove the starboard gunwale beneath the surface, and the sea poured in. Ice-cold water swallowed our little dinghy in one long, merciless gulp.

Everything slowed down—the swoosh of water over the gunwales, the boat sinking beneath us, Neil's wide eyes meeting mine in mutual disbelief. The cold hit my body like a thousand needles, instant and bone-deep.

Could this really be happening? Right now? On this day of all days?

"We're going down, Neil!"

There was nothing to do but abandon ship—full foul-weather gear, boots and all—and swim for shore. I grabbed the bow line with one hand and kicked with everything I had, dragging the swamped dinghy behind me while the frigid water burned every inch of my body. Neil splashed alongside me, and together we finally reached the beach, hauling the dinghy onto the sand before collapsing beside it.

From the dock came the sound I had dreaded: laughter.

The salty fishermen who had been watching our departure were now doubled over, enjoying the show. Salty John stood among them, a flat of fresh bunker in his arms, watching the whole display. He turned to another lobsterman beside him.

"This freaking kid doesn't stand a chance, eh?"

And then something remarkable happened.

John cracked a smile—perhaps the first one in years.

"Holy crap, that was cold!" Neil said, shivering beside me on the sand.

I looked at him and shook my head. "I can't believe that just happened. How embarrassing."

But there was nothing to do except laugh.

And so we did.

I called my Dad, and thankfully, he arrived shortly after with dry clothes and hot coffee—and, of course, he couldn't resist.

"Here, son," he said, barely containing his grin. "I brought you a change of clothes. Also brought a floatie, in case you need it."

Neil and I dried off, warmed up, and gathered ourselves. Then we walked down to the dock and welcomed our waiting customers aboard as if nothing had happened.

The mood was light. Everyone was smiling. The day went on.

I guess life knew that, to get through the adventure ahead, I definitely was going to need a sense of humor. And so began my very first trip as a captain of my own boat—for better or worse—aboard the *Celtic Quest*.

25

DAY 1

Now that Neil and I were done entertaining the locals with our little "sinking dinghy" routine, we had peeled off our soaked clothes, pulled on warm, dry ones, and managed to laugh it off. It was time to get back to the task at hand.

"Come on, folks!" I motioned to the customers waiting patiently at the end of the dock. "Come on down! Welcome aboard the Celtic Quest."

The first two to stomp down the ramp were Bobby and Tommy, old friends from my days working the boats in Port Jeff. They were jovial, fun-loving guys, but they were also professionally trained ball-busters. They'd always promised that if I ever got my own boat, they'd be there to support me. True to their word, here they were—they had no intention of letting me off easy.

"Wow, Des, this is a… um… this is a really nice boat you have," Bobby said.

They were trying to be polite, but the hesitation said it all. I caught their eyes scanning the deck. The Celtic Quest was humble, to say the least. She was an old wooden boat—barebones, no cabin, and equipped with a tiny toilet that required a prayer to flush. Despite the month Dad and I had spent scrubbing, painting, and toiling in the shipyard, we couldn't hide the years of hard work she had already endured. She wasn’t a yacht, but she was proud. And she was mine.

“I know, guys, she’s humble,” I said, touching the cap rail. “But I promise she is safe.”

“Okay, you sure this thing floats?” Tommy asked, shooting a grin at Neil.

“Yeah, my Dad and I just spent a month in the shipyard making sure of it. Hop on. Trust me.”

Bobby paused with one foot on the rail. “Des, if we don't make it home, you are in charge of calling my wife, okay?”

“Very funny, Bob.”

“All right, would you get on the dang boat already and let the other people through? You're holding up the line.”

“Whoa, whoa, easy, Cap. You can't talk to your customers like that,” Bobby laughed, finally stepping aboard. He knew I was kidding; we’d been talking to each other like that for years.

Behind them were the only other two customers for the day: a nicely dressed man named James and his son, a boy of about ten. The father didn’t look much like a fisherman—he looked more like a tourist who had decided on a whim to treat his kid to an adventure—and I was glad to have them aboard.

We loaded up, cast off the lines, and headed out into the Sound. Thankfully, there wasn't a wave on the water.

As I throttled up and pointed the bow toward the grounds, an amazing feeling washed over me. I looked out east toward the rising sun, the water shimmering gold and calm. I took a quiet moment to look up and thank God for finally bringing me to this place. This was the dream I’d had since I was a little boy cruising the harbor with my brother in our skiff. I was finally here.

We arrived at the grounds and anchored up at our coordinates. It wasn't long before I heard the first call.

“Captain! Net!”

I looked down from the helm. Bobby had snagged the first bite and was doubled over the rail.

“I got it!” I yelled.

I grabbed the net and scrambled down to the deck. Bobby hauled up a beautiful five-pound blackfish—the first legal fish ever caught on the Celtic Quest.

"First fish on the boat!" I announced.

The bite was on. Rods started bending all along the rails. Even the young boy got in on the action. He struggled against the weight of the rod, his face a mask of pure concentration, until he finally hauled a blackfish over the rail.

When I unhooked it and handed it to him, the kid's face lit up with a huge smile. His Dad stepped in close and wrapped an arm around his shoulder, both of them grinning ear to ear. I snapped a photo—one I knew they'd treasure long after the fish was gone.

By the end of the trip, we had put together a solid catch. Neil worked hard on the deck, filleting fish and joking with the passengers. We disembarked the customers, washed down the decks, and put the old girl back on her mooring.

"This was a really great day with my son," James told me later, shaking my hand. "Thank you."

"Day one in the books, Neil. And what a fine day it was."

"Des, I'm so happy for you," Neil said. "It was a real pleasure seeing you run your own boat."

"Thanks, Neil. I've got to say—it feels good. It really does."

"Now," Neil added, eyeing the water, "we still have to get back to shore in this darn dinghy of yours."

We both burst out laughing.

"Well, let's hope this row goes a little better than this morning did."

"Ah, Des, I don't think you and I are ever going to live that one down."

"No," I said, climbing carefully into the tiny boat. "I'm sure the salty locals are all chuckling at the bar right now, telling their friends about the punk kid who thinks he can run a fishing boat out of their harbor."

As I rowed us toward the beach—successfully this time—Neil looked at me. He was an old, salty Captain with a long career behind him, and in the fading light, he gave me a slow, solid nod. It felt like respect. Like he might've been seeing a younger version of himself.

"Let's hope that's the first of many great trips," he said.

"I sure hope so, Neil."

We tied up the dinghy, I packed up my truck—still buzzing with adrenaline—and headed home. I burst through the front door smiling. The smell of pot roast hit me immediately. Mom was in the kitchen. She was an incredible cook, and nobody could put together a hearty meal after a hard day's work like her.

"Day one in the books, Mom!"

"So proud and happy for you, Des." She wiped her hands on her apron and pulled me into one of those hugs only a mother can give. "Your father told me about your little swim this morning."

"Of course he did," I groaned. "No way he's ever letting that one go."

"You know it's all in good fun. Besides your polar plunge, how did the rest of the day go?"

"You mean once we dried off?" I smiled. "It went great, Mom. Awesome day. Great people. Plenty of fish. It was special."

"I'm so happy to hear that. I was thinking about you all day, praying everything went well."

"Thanks, Mom. Your prayers definitely work."

She smiled and turned back to the oven. "Do you have anyone booked for tomorrow?"

My stomach did a small flip. "That's a great question. I'm going to check right now."

I hurried down to the far end of the house where I'd set up my "office." It wasn't much—just a white plastic table shoved into the corner of my bedroom and an unforgiving wooden chair. Sitting on the desk was my cutting-edge technology: an answering machine with a blinking light.

I walked in, expecting to see it flashing wildly.

It wasn't blinking.

"What the heck?" I tapped the machine. "Is this thing on? Zero calls?"

I sat down, the adrenaline draining out of me. "Surely someone must've called."

I dialed my own number from the other line. The machine picked up immediately, clear as day, recording my test message without a hiccup. It wasn't broken.

I checked the caller ID. The last call had come in at 10:00 p.m. the night before.

"Really?" I muttered. "Zero customers?"

I slumped back. "Well… I guess Day Two is postponed."

I called Neil to give him the update.

"Actually, Neil… so far we've got zero calls for any upcoming trips."

"Really? After all the advertising you did?"

"Yeah. I thought people would be calling." I tried to mask the disappointment, but I knew he could hear it. "This might be a longer slog than I expected."

"Don't get ahead of yourself," Neil said calmly. "I'm ready when you are. Just keep me posted."

"Thanks, Neil. I appreciate it."

I hung up and took a deep breath, trying to shake the weight in my chest.

"Ah, it's just one day," I said aloud to the empty room. "Tomorrow will be better."

Fishermen are funny creatures. They only want to fish with captains they trust, and trust takes time. I knew building a customer base would be a grind—I just hadn't realized how steep that grind might feel at the beginning.

But for now, I was going to enjoy Mom's pot roast and celebrate day one.

At least that part went right.

26

COME HELL OR HIGH WATER

UNFORTUNATELY, THE TREND CONTINUED, AND DAYS WOULD GO BY without a single phone call. On many a day, I slumped into my office chair and stared at that stupid glowing zero. If they'd designed a number to perfectly summarize my bank account, my reservation list, and my emotional state all at once, this was it.

Over the next month, I scraped together a few profitable trips, but most days were break-even at best—and more often, solidly in the red. I'd show up at the dock hopeful and see two, maybe three people waiting to sail on a boat that could easily handle many more.

Every time, that familiar wave of frustration hit—the instant, gut-level, *you've got to be kidding me* feeling. And every time, I forced myself to shake it off.

"Just going fishing," I'd mutter under my breath. "Going to treat these folks to the best day they've ever had. That's all I can do."

Eventually, things got so tight that I had to swallow my pride and take a side job running one of the other local fishing boats a few days a week.

The first morning I showed up on that competitor's boat wearing their company T-shirt, one of the regulars did a double-take.

"Des?" he said. "What are you doing here? Didn't you start your own boat?"

He'd fished with me back in Port Jeff—had even come out on the Celtic Quest once or twice. A good guy. And right then, he looked... almost embarrassed for me.

I forced a small smile. "Yeah. Things are just a bit slow right now, so I'm helping out over here."

That sentence stung every single time I said it.

He nodded, but his eyes said the rest: *Wow. It's not really going so well for Des and his new boat.*

I turned back to the wheel, gripped it tight, and focused on the job ahead. If I were going to run someone else's boat, I was going to do it right. Customers didn't care whose name was on the paperwork—they just wanted a good day on the water. And that, at least, I could still give them.

But inside, I was fighting—fighting to stay proud of what I'd tried to build, fighting not to feel like I was already failing.

By the end of that month, things were sliding into crisis mode. Loans maxed. Credit cards maxed. Cash? None. Every dollar that came across the rail in fare money went straight into diesel, bait, tackle, and keeping the boat alive one more week.

My business wasn't just struggling—it was on life support.

One more bad blow, I knew, and I'd be done.

Unfortunately, that blow came the very next morning.

I rode out to the Celtic Quest in our little aluminum dinghy like I always did, trying not to think too much. The harbor was peaceful. The boat sat steady on the mooring, looking solid, almost reassuring.

I climbed aboard, stowed the dinghy, and went through my usual routine. Down into the engine room: oil checked. Water levels checked. Belts tight. Bilges clear. Everything looked normal.

Back up to the wheelhouse.

I slid into the Captain's chair like I'd done a thousand times. Reached forward. Put my hand on the key.

I didn't say anything out loud. But deep down, there was a quiet plea.

Not today. Please. Not today.

I turned the key.

The engine made a terrible grinding, rattling sound.

For a moment, I froze there with my hand still on the key, in disbelief at what I just heard. I felt my heart rate spike as my thoughts raced ahead.

There's no way. There's no freaking way my engine crapped out. It just can't be. Not now. Not with no money. Not with everything already hanging by a thread.

I closed my eyes and took a long, slow breath, trying to reel my thoughts back in. But the sinking feeling in the pit of my stomach was heavy and unmistakable.

I opened my eyes and stared at the dead gauges, my hand still resting on the useless key.

There was nothing left to throw at this. No money. No credit. No margin for error.

Just a broken engine—and a boat that wasn't going anywhere.

I JUMPED down into the engine room to start assessing the damage. When I finally pulled the dipstick and held it up to the light, my stomach dropped. Metal shavings glittered in the oil like tiny fragments of my future falling apart. I pulled one of the inspection plates off the side of the engine block to look a little closer and confirmed what I had feared. One of the cylinders had let go. Catastrophic failure. The entire motor would have to come apart.

I threw my tools on the deck and pulled my oily body up out of the bilge. My deckhand Phil was standing there watching, and I could see the fear in his young face. He knew something was seriously wrong.

"Goddamn engine is toast," I said. "Totally shot. Done. I thought I heard something when I was putting her on the mooring yesterday, and she'd been running a little hot, but I had no idea it was this bad."

"I'm so sorry, Des. What are you going to do?"

"Honestly, I have no idea." I looked down at my oil-covered hands and felt the weight of everything pressing down on me. "I have no money. We have no business to speak of. I'm broke, and now this."

"Is there anything I can do to help?"

"No. We're screwed for good, I'm pretty sure."

Phil didn't respond. There was no point in saying any more. My heart was breaking, and he knew it.

I sat down on the gunwale and stared at my blackened hands and feet. "What a kick in the ass this is," I mumbled.

After a few more minutes lost in my daze, I gathered my gear and drove home. My parents could tell something was wrong the moment I opened the door.

"Des, you okay?"

"Actually, no, Dad. Can I talk to you?"

A parent always knows when their child is really hurting.

I sat down at the kitchen table, still wearing my soiled clothes, my boots still on. I hadn't mustered the energy to change. My father sat across from me, waiting.

"Dad, you're not going to believe this, but I blew my engine today."

"You what?"

"I blew my engine. One of the pistons is toast. The whole motor has to come apart. I'm screwed."

"My God. I'm sorry, Des. What are you going to do?"

"Honestly, Dad, I have no idea." I felt my voice start to crack. "I don't think I can do this anymore. For months, I've been busting my tail, doing my best, sailing out with two or three people a day. Each week, I'm going deeper into debt. I have no idea how I'm going to pay all this money back. And now my engine goes? Do you know how much that costs? I just can't keep doing this."

My father let me finish. Then he spoke.

"Son, lift your head up and look at me."

I raised my eyes to meet his, and what I saw there steadied me. There was strength in those eyes, the kind that comes from having walked through fire and come out the other side. He had lost his career as a firefighter to injury, rebuilt his life from scratch, and raised a family through thick and thin. He knew something about setbacks and about paths forward.

"You're going to get through this," he said. "I know you will. But right now, in this moment, you're shot. You're exhausted and frustrated. Just take a breath and try to calm down. Please, son—get yourself a hot shower and some sleep. We can talk about it tomorrow, but right now is not the time for you to make a decision like this. Okay?"

His strength was a comfort.

"Okay, Dad. Okay. You're right."

Slowly, I made my way to the bathroom, kicked off my oily boots and clothes, and took a hot shower. Then I lay down in bed and pulled the blankets over my head.

I tossed and turned for hours, unable to sleep, my mind consumed with anger and disappointment. I felt like I had let myself down. I had never thought I would fail at something like this. But I was digging myself into a hole that kept getting deeper, and at some point, you have to admit defeat. At some point, you have to say you gave it your all and it just wasn't meant to be.

By the time I finally drifted off around three in the morning, I had resigned myself to the fact that tomorrow I would wake up and possibly close down my business.

I opened my eyes at first light, and my first thought hit me like a punch.

Crap. That wasn't a dream.

I sat up on the edge of my bed, heart heavy, and my eyes drifted to the picture on the wall. My mother had framed it for me after opening day—a photograph she'd taken of me sailing out of the harbor on that first trip, the morning sun burning gold on the horizon behind me. She had captured something in that image, some proud and hopeful version of myself heading out to meet the future, and she had been kind enough to frame it so I would always remember.

I stared at that picture for a long time.

And then I thought of all the other people who might come to fish with me someday, if only I could find a way to keep going.

As much as I felt like a failure, as hard as this blow had landed, did I really want to give up after coming this far?

I could feel something stirring in my belly. Not the anger and frustration of the night before, but something deeper. A fire. A resolve that rose up from somewhere I didn't know I had.

I pounded the bed with my fist and stood up.

"No way in hell I'm quitting. No way."

I pulled on my clothes, stepped into my boots, and made my way to the kitchen, where my Mom and Dad were having breakfast. Dad looked up and saw that I was heading for the door.

"Morning, son. How are you feeling? Where are you going?"

"I'm going fishing, Dad. No way I'm quitting. I'm going fishing."

He looked stunned. "Wow, really? You're really going to try to get through this?"

"I sure am. Come hell or high water." I grabbed my gear and headed for the door. "But first, I have a boat to fix."

I hopped in my truck and drove back to the marina, talking to myself the whole way so my mind wouldn't stray to fear.

"I'm going to find a way. Somehow, I'm going to find a way."

27

WHERE THERE IS A WILL, THERE IS A WAY

As I pulled into the marina, I spotted Barbara walking down the dock. Barbara was a small, gritty elderly woman with short, curly gray hair who carried herself with an air of confidence and self-reliance that came from having lived a full and difficult life. She had run this marina for decades—through disasters, setbacks, and the daily grind of keeping a business alive on the water.

Only a few years earlier, she had lost her husband and lifelong partner to Alzheimer's, watching the man she loved disappear piece by piece. And yet she still showed up every day with a warm smile and that depth in her eyes that only comes from having walked through life's trials and found a way to keep going.

"Hi, Barbara. Good morning," I called as she approached.

"What's with the long face, Des? You're usually so chipper."

"Barbara, I blew my engine."

"Oh," she said softly. "I'm so sorry, Des. Goodness."

"Yeah, it sucks. I'm doing my best to find a way through this, but I just don't know what to do."

She studied me for a moment. "You know, I've been watching you sail past my dock every few days with just a couple of people on board. I was wondering how the heck you were going to hold on with no money coming in. And now this?"

"Yup," I said. "I think I'm screwed."

Barbara looked at me with those knowing eyes of hers, and when she spoke, her voice carried the weight of everything she had lived through.

"You know what, Des? You may very well be screwed." She paused, holding my gaze. "But I've been watching you play around this harbor and on these docks since you were a little kid. I remember you and your brother zipping around in that little boat, showing up at my bait shop to buy clams and bunker before heading out on your adventures. I saw the joy in you boys. I knew even then that you had something special."

She smiled gently. "You were different, Des. You were meant to be a fisherman."

She leaned in just a bit. "You *can* do this. Where there's a will, there's a way. Never stop believing that. You hear me?"

I didn't say anything. I just stood there, deeply moved by the strength of her words and the conviction in her eyes. It was exactly what I needed to hear in that moment.

I thanked her and walked slowly down the dock, her words reverberating in my mind. I asked several of the other boat owners if they knew anyone who could help me with the engine. And somehow—through the quiet network of fishermen and marina folks who look out for their own—I was led to a mechanic named Woody.

Woody was a legend in our world, as salty as they come, a man who had been working on marine diesels for over four decades. He'd lost one of his fingers somewhere along the way, but it hadn't slowed him down one bit. He always wore dark blue mechanic's clothes, and his fingernails permanently carried that faint trace of oil no amount of scrubbing could remove.

When I explained my situation—broke, desperate, facing a full engine rebuild—he just nodded and said, "Let's take a look."

We pulled the engine apart together, and when it finally came time to talk about money, Woody looked at me and said five words I will never forget:

"Just pay me whenever, kid."

Woody and I worked tirelessly together from the crack of dawn till dusk, methodically pulling the engine apart and then slowly rebuilding it. I stood by his side, fetched whatever tools he needed, and did my best to support him. He was a master technician who knew every part of that engine by heart after a lifetime of working on these big diesels. He never complained. He never wavered. He just kept his head down and worked tirelessly until the job was done. He truly was the angel I needed in that moment.

A FEW WEEKS LATER, my phone rang. It was my sister, Kait. She was a talented artist who scraped together every nickel she earned selling her work. I had been too proud to ask her for help, knowing how hard she worked for her money. Somehow, she had heard about my troubles and was calling to offer me a loan to help keep me afloat.

I don't think she realized how close I had come to giving up. But her call, arriving exactly when it did, felt like grace showing up unannounced.

With Kait's loan, I was able to start paying Woody back, put fuel in the boat, and bought some fresh bait. By the grace of God, I was back in business.

Now came the real test. Business before the breakdown had been almost nonexistent. I had to find a way to get people back on the boat.

I called everyone I could think of to tell them we were back in business. I posted pictures online, sent emails, and placed a fresh ad in the paper—throwing everything I had into one last push.

And despite all the uncertainty, I could feel something shifting. The tide was changing. I could feel it in my bones.

During the weeks we worked on the engine, the weather had cooled, and the water temperature dropped. This was the time of year fishermen wait for—the fall run—when some of the best fishing of the entire season comes alive. It felt like my last real shot at turning things around.

I showed up early on our first day back, filled with anticipation.

"Well, how many people do we have today?" I asked Phil as I climbed out of my truck.

He hesitated. "Um, Cap… we only have two people."

"Two fares? That's it?"

After everything I'd been through—after all the calls, the effort, the fighting to get back on the water—I bowed my head for a moment and felt the familiar negative voices starting to creep in.

Then I shook my head and snapped out of it.

"You know what? I don't care. We're going fishing. We're going to take these two people out and give them the best day of their lives. That's all we can do."

Phil nodded. "Sounds good to me, Cap. Let's just go fishing."

And just like I'd hoped, the fall run was on.

What a day it was.

I took them to one of my best spots—and it was absolutely loaded. We caught so many fish that we headed back early because the customers said they'd had enough. As they climbed off the boat, one of them grabbed my hand and shook it hard.

"Cap, that was the best day of fishing I've ever had. I can't wait to tell all my friends."

"Sure was an amazing day, fellas," I said. "Can't wait to see you again."

They must have told a lot of people—because the very next morning, they were back. And this time, they brought a whole gang of fishing buddies with them. Many were names I recognized from the local online fishing forums. Though the internet was still young, these guys were some of the most active fishermen around, constantly sharing reports and tips.

They had contacted each other in one of the online forums the night prior, and word got out that the little boat in Mount Sinai Harbor had caught a ton of fish.

The fishing was incredible again—a perfect repeat of the day before. Once again, they were blown away by the caliber of fishing and promised to be back. And once again, they told all their friends.

I rushed home afterward to post another report, and when I walked into my room and saw the little plastic desk in the corner, I stopped cold.

The red light on my answering machine was flashing.

The display read: "Answering machine full."

I stared at it, stunned. I had never seen that message before. For a moment, I wondered if the machine was broken.

It wasn't.

I sat down and started playing the messages one after another, writing down names and numbers as a huge smile spread across my face. People were calling from near and far, asking to book trips on my boat. By the time I returned the calls, the next day was completely sold out.

We went out again and put together another incredible catch. The customers were thrilled—and they told even more people.

The fishing stayed hot for weeks, and word kept spreading about the little boat in Mount Sinai. Coming home to a full answering machine became normal. We sailed every single day for the rest of the season, completely sold out.

By the time the season ended, I had saved enough money to pay back Woody and my sister Kait—with enough left over to get through the winter.

This was the turning point.

We were going to make it.

28

A SPECIAL TIME

My cell phone rang in the middle of Mom's pot roast dinner. It was early the following spring, and the three of us were sitting around the kitchen table the way we always did, Dad enjoying my Mom's fine cooking, while my Mom listened to one of the many old war stories he loved to tell. I looked down at the screen and saw my brother's name.

"Des," John said. "I got some time before my coaching job starts. What do you say I come down and work with you for the spring black-fish season? Help you get going. And on the days you don't have customers, we can go fishing together for old times' sake. Find some new spots. Just have a great time."

I didn't even hesitate. I said yes before he finished the sentence.

When I hung up and told my parents, Mom's face lit up the way it always did when it came to her firstborn. "John-o!" she said, already halfway out of her chair in spirit. "It would be so great to have him home. I'll make up his room, make sure he has nice, clean sheets, and that he's fed well. I can't wait to see him!"

Dad just smiled and shook his head a little, the way he did when something quietly moved him, but he wasn't going to make a fuss about it.

John had always been the athlete in the family. He played soccer at a level most people only dream about, captaining the men's team at Fordham and then turning professional for a stretch after college. But the body can only take so much punishment at that pace, and years of nagging injuries had finally caught up with him. He made the difficult decision to step away from playing and answer a different calling—coaching and mentoring the next generation of players. He had spent the last several years coaching Division 1 soccer for the University of Vermont, but he had now accepted a new job running a youth club in Michigan, which he wouldn't have to begin until the end of May.

I was in the middle of my second season running Celtic Quest out of Mount Sinai, having survived a very trying first season. But the truth was, I still could barely afford to pay a crew. The idea of having my big brother at my side—one of the best fishermen and deckhands I'd ever known, the person who had trained me on the water when I was just a kid, and not to mention my best friend—was almost too good to be true.

When John arrived, and I brought him down to the boat for the first time, I watched his face carefully as he took it all in. Celtic Quest was no luxury vessel. She was a humble, no-frills working boat, narrow in the beam with a cramped deck layout that made moving around a chore, and a head that barely functioned on its best day and needed constant tending. The passage up to the bow was tight and awkward, barely wide enough for a man to squeeze through with any gear in his hands.

But the real moment of reckoning came when John walked up to the bow and got his first look at the anchoring situation. The bow pulpit was a rickety piece of oak that had been baking in the salt and sun for the better part of fifty years, cracked and dry-rotted, with a small twenty-five-pound anchor dangling off the front that was nowhere near sufficient for the kind of fishing we did in the Sound. Our actual anchors weighed over fifty pounds each, built heavy to hold bottom in the hard current and sticky mud we worked in most days. With the inadequate pulpit, we just had to hang those heavy anchors by hand over the brass railings on the bow.

John looked at the setup, then looked at me, and said, "Wait. There's no anchor hauler?"

I shrugged my shoulders and gave him the most apologetic look I could manage. "Yeah, no. Sorry. I guess I didn't mention that part. We pull the anchors by hand."

He just stared at me for a second, processing what he had signed up for. Then he turned to me with a bit of a smirk. "So I guess you're just trying to get even with me. For all those years, I had you do free labor?"

We both laughed, but he knew I didn't have the money yet to invest in a hydraulic system, which would cost thousands of dollars that I simply didn't have. That upgrade would have to wait until I put a few more dollars in the bank. In the meantime, I had my brother's back and arms, and I was grateful for both.

John dove in with all his heart, the way he did with everything. The spring blackfish season came on strong, thank God, and we were now carrying enough people to sail consistently. John was a natural on deck—quick, capable, and genuinely warm with people—and the customers loved him. He did well earning tips, which helped put a few extra dollars in his pocket on top of the modest wage I was able to pay him. It was a win for both of us.

We fell into a rhythm together that felt just like old times. On the days we had customers, we worked hard and fished hard. And on the days we didn't have enough fares to justify a trip, we did what we had always done best—we went fishing, of course.

As luck would have it, the government had recently completed a massive marine survey of Long Island Sound for navigation purposes and had published, for the first time ever, a database of coordinates for every sunken wreck they'd discovered on the bottom. To a fisherman, a sunken wreck is an absolute gold mine. Wrecks provide homes and shelter for crabs, sea life, and baitfish, which in turn attract the predator fish that feed on them. Blackfish especially love to live in wrecks, tucking themselves into every crevice and hollow. When you find one that's never been fished before, it is one of the ultimate experiences a Captain can have.

On bad-weather days, John and I sat around my parents' house, plotting all the new wrecks from that database, studying my charts and marking coordinates, and planning which ones to hit first. We had our eye on a cluster of drops way up near the Connecticut coastline that sat in what looked like absolutely prime blackfish territory. We'd been waiting for our moment.

It came on a gray morning in early May. A light east wind was rolling down the Sound, and a steady drizzle had kept the customers away. John and I came downstairs to find Mom already in the kitchen, and she offered to make us breakfast before we headed out. Bacon and eggs—who turns that down? Dad came down and joined us, too, and I spread my chart out across the dining room table with all my marks on it, the Connecticut wrecks circled in red.

"We're going to go find those wrecks up on the Connecticut side," I told him.

Dad looked at the chart, looked out the window at the weather, and shook his head a little. "The boys are crazy going out there today."

"It's just what we do, Dad," we told him.

Those wrecks were fifteen to twenty miles from the dock, which was the furthest I had ever taken my humble little boat, but we were ready for the adventure. We wolfed down breakfast, grabbed our gear and our rods, and headed for the water.

After a two-hour steam, we only had to search for a few minutes to find the first one. A big sunken barge, over a hundred feet long, sitting in the perfect depth for blackfish. I stayed in the wheelhouse as the anchor lines came tight, watching my coordinates on the screen to make sure we were positioned just right. But John, of course, had already grabbed his rod and made the first cast before I could even step outside.

I heard him yelling from the stern. "Sea bass!"

I ran out just in time to see him swing a beautiful jumbo over the rail, grinning like a kid who had just opened the best present of his life. I grabbed my rod and dropped my bait to the bottom alongside his, and we both hooked up at the same time, standing side by side, reeling in gorgeous blackfish and laughing the whole way up. We were like children at Christmas, hardly able to believe what we had found—this glory hole so many miles from the dock that nobody had ever fished before. We filled the tote in no time.

Then I looked at John and said, "Let's go find the next one. There's another wreck just a mile or two from here."

We pulled anchors and ran to the next set of coordinates, and another massive sunken structure popped up on the fish finder. Our eyes went wide. We just looked at each other like we couldn't believe our luck. Another enormous wreck, right there, loaded with fish. We anchored up and started whaling on them all over again.

Only this time, that light east wind that had seemed so harmless in the morning forecast was starting to build. What had been a gentle two-foot roll was now a steady four to five feet, and the waves were stacking up with real authority. Almost twenty miles from home in my humble little boat, this was starting to concern me. But we were so locked in, so full of adrenaline and joy, that we just tightened up our foul-weather gear, put our heads down, and kept fishing, swinging in fish after fish, laughing and smiling at each other through the rain.

Another half-hour passed, and the wind was now howling over twenty-five knots out of the east as a low-pressure front pushed in, turning the Sound into a churning mess. Finally, as I was reeling in yet another fish, I looked at John and said, "Brother, I can't believe I'm saying this. This is some of the greatest fishing of our lives, but we have got to get the hell out of here. This is getting terrible."

John nodded. "Yeah, you ain't kidding, brother. I think we'd better get headed for home."

We pulled the anchors and turned tail to the southwest. The waves were off our stern quarter, which meant we could ride with them rather than pound into them, but the wind had climbed past thirty knots now and the seas were still building. My little boat with her single diesel barely made eight knots on a good day, and she was riding up on the face of these swells and then surfing down the front of them before torquing sideways with a sickening creak in the trough. Each time she corkscrewed, you could hear the old fasteners being pushed to their limit—that sound like a creaky old wooden door that hasn't been oiled in years, groaning as it closes. I'd spin the wheel to straighten her out, and then do it all over again on the next wave.

I had spent the previous winter redoing that entire hull—taken her down to bare wood, re-caulked every seam, sealed everything with fresh epoxy—and now, feeling her twist and groan beneath me for nearly two hours, I was praying that all that work would hold.

We didn't say much on the ride home. We just rode it out.

When we finally made our way back through the jetties into the safe waters of Mount Sinai Harbor, Dad was already waiting in the parking lot at the commercial boat ramp. He knew the weather had turned bad. We could see him from the water, waving as we pulled in, eager to make sure we were okay. He came walking down the floating dock toward us, and we yelled out to him before he even reached the boat.

"Dad, you won't believe the fishing trip we just had!"

His eyes lit up the way they always did when fishing was involved.

"We found a couple of brand-new wrecks loaded with fish and absolutely killed them!"

John reached into the tote and held up one of the beautiful big blackfish we had caught. Dad broke into a wide smile as he came closer, but then he slowed down and stopped in his tracks about twenty feet from the bow. The smile faded, and a look of real concern came over his face.

"What is it, Dad?"

He just stood there for a second, not saying anything. Then he slowly raised his hand and pointed at the hull, and looked back at us with worry all over his face.

"What the hell did you do to your boat?"

"What are you talking about?" I shouted back.

"Son," he said quietly, "you'd better come see this."

I jumped off the boat, walked up to the bow, and my heart sank. Every seam I had so carefully caulked and sanded smooth as a baby's bottom was blown wide open. The endless corkscrewing and torquing as we came down the face of those waves had twisted my old boat so hard that all that meticulous work—hours and hours of it—was completely destroyed. The bow looked like hell. I put my hand on my head and just stood there shaking it. I couldn't believe what I was looking at.

I turned to John, looking for some kind of encouragement, I

suppose. He just put his hands up, gave a little shrug, and said, "I'm sorry, brother."

Structurally, the boat was still sound. We weren't taking on excess water or anything like that. It was cosmetic more than anything. But I had taken such pride in making her shine, and now she looked like she'd been through a war.

Dad read the moment carefully, the way good fathers do. He waited a beat, then gently tested the waters. "Well," he said, with a long, careful pause, "aside from all that... did you boys enjoy yourselves at all?"

And just like that, John and I snapped out of it. We looked at each other and broke into huge smiles. "Hell yeah, Dad. One of the best trips of our lives."

That evening, we sat around the kitchen table together—Mom shaking her head a little at our story, though after years of dragging her along on our adventures as kids, she understood. She was just glad we were home and okay, and she could see how happy we were. That's all a parent really wants, I think. And the more we talked, the bigger the fish got, the way fish stories always go. Dad asked questions. Mom refilled our glasses. John and I kept looking at each other, both of us knowing that what we'd found out there was something we would never forget.

"That was one hell of a bad ride home," John finally said, "but I gotta tell you—that was worth it, man."

He put his hand up for a high five. I slapped it and said, "Couldn't agree more. Catching fish like that, finding new wrecks—nothing beats it. I'll figure out a way to fix the bow with some epoxy and paint, and we'll fish another day."

When the spring season finally ended, John packed up his car to head back to Michigan and begin his new coaching job. The morning he left, the three of us stood on the front porch—me, Mom, and Dad—and watched him load the last of his bags. We gave each other big hugs, the kind where nobody lets go first, and then John got in and slowly pulled out of the driveway. We stood there waving until the car disappeared down the street.

I looked at my parents, and all three of us were a little teary-eyed.

"Gonna miss my brother," I said.

Dad put his arm around me. "I am too, son. He's a good man. Hopefully, we'll see him again soon."

I knew, even as I watched him drive away, that what we'd had together those weeks was something we would never quite have again. John was starting a new career and a new chapter of his life, moving far from home, and the kind of time we'd just shared—two brothers fishing the Sound every day like they were kids again—that doesn't come around twice. But it came around once. And standing there on the porch with my Mom and Dad, watching the driveway where John's car had just been, I said it quietly to myself.

I'll always remember this.

29

MOM'S MAGIC

One of the gifts I never foresaw when I dreamed of starting a fishing business was how deeply it would weave itself into my family's life. The boat became more than a livelihood. It became a place where the people I loved could step into my world and share it with me, and that turned out to be worth more than any paycheck.

Dad came out with me often that summer after John left, eager to learn about navigation and how to handle the boat, asking questions the way he always did when something genuinely interested him. He loved being out there, and I loved having him.

My Mom also loved to come aboard, though she usually arrived with a guest or two in tow, someone fascinating she had befriended with her uncanny gift for meeting extraordinary people wherever she went. Everyone was fascinating to my Mom, and I mean everyone. She saw the light and wonder in even the most ordinary of people and situations, a true earth angel who moved through the world with her heart wide open and her arms even wider.

In our family, it was a running joke that wherever we went, Mom would inevitably disappear for a while and come back beaming, saying, "You will never believe this, but I just met the most fascinating person!" Growing up, she had visitors staying with us from all around the world. You never knew who was coming through the door next. We had guests from Germany, France, England, Ireland, Yugoslavia, Russia, China. Doctors, artists, philosophers, missionaries, politicians. Our house was a revolving door of humanity, and Mom was the one holding it open.

Once she came bursting through the front door and announced, "Guys! You will never believe who is coming to visit today. A real Masai warrior chief who came all the way from Kenya to see us!" And sure enough, she had in fact befriended a real Masai chief, adorned head to toe in his traditional jewelry and carrying his staff. He had come to the States to raise money for his tribe, and of course, Mom had offered to help him out. Of course she had.

Another day, Dad was cleaning out some shelves in the pantry when a brick fell off the shelf and hit him on the head.

"What the heck was that!" Dad yelled, rubbing the spot where it caught him.

"Oh, I'm sorry, Desmond," Mom said calmly. "That's just a piece of the Berlin Wall."

Dad rubbed his head for another second, then turned to her and started laughing. "Ah, Kathy. I must say, it is definitely never dull living with you."

That was Mom. Wherever she went, she sprinkled her fairy dust, and magic just seemed to unfold around her. She was used to it. She expected it. And the rest of us had long since learned to just hold on and enjoy the ride.

So when she came into the living room one summer evening while I was stretched out on the couch watching a Yankee game, I should have known by the size of her smile that something interesting was coming.

"Des, I have the most wonderful and unusual guests to bring on your boat," she said, practically glowing.

I sat up a little and braced myself for the big reveal.

"I have the high priest and twelve of his top students from one of the most famous martial arts monasteries in China, and they would like to go fishing with you. Most of them have never even been on a boat before. Will you take them?"

I looked at her for a long beat. A high priest and twelve martial arts monks from a Chinese monastery. On my boat. In Mount Sinai Harbor. Nothing about my mother surprised me anymore, but I had to admit, this was a new one.

"What? Um, OK. Sure, Mom."

Apparently, they had come to the States to raise money for their monastery, and somehow my mother had, of course, befriended them along the way. When they mentioned that they had never even been on a boat, she just had to offer.

"I hope that's OK," she said with that familiar sparkle in her eye.

"Of course I'll take them, Mom. I love being part of your crazy adventures." I gave her a hug and tried not to think too hard about the logistics of fitting a high priest, twelve monks, my mother, and my father onto my humble little fishing boat.

The following day, before our fishing trip, Mom took me to the martial arts demonstration they were performing at a local conference center. A couple of hundred people filled the seats, and when the high priest walked out onto the stage, the room fell silent.

He moved across the floor in flowing silk robes, his hair tucked in a bun, gliding with a grace and stillness that seemed to bend the air around him. And then he began to move. What followed was the most mind-boggling display of acrobatic martial arts I had ever seen a human being perform, a lifetime of training made visible in every gesture, every strike, every impossible leap and landing. This was a man who had spent his entire life cultivating his body, mind, and soul through the artistry of movement and mindfulness, and it showed in ways that left you speechless.

One by one, he invited his students to join him, and they took the stage with swords, staffs, and knives, running and jumping and flipping through the air with a confidence and precision that was equal parts beautiful and terrifying. The audience sat there in stunned silence, watching these men wield deadly weapons with the ease of someone turning a page in a book.

I leaned over to my Mom and whispered, "Oh my God, Mom. These are the people I have to take fishing today? What the heck did you get me into?" She gave me a playful elbow to the ribs and just smiled. But sitting there watching these warriors perform feats that defied what I thought a human body could do, I couldn't help but laugh to myself at the absurdity of what was about to happen. I was going to load these men onto my little fishing boat in Mount Sinai Harbor and hand them rods and reels. It was almost too much to process.

After the performance, they had some lunch, and then we all headed down to the commercial dock at the harbor. It was a working afternoon on the water, and several of the local lobster boats were tied up along the dock as their crews finished unloading the day's catch. Totes of lobsters were being dragged down the planks, and the air was thick with the familiar smell of bunker and herring that always hung around the dock.

The martial artists stepped out of their vehicles in their beautiful silk robes and slippers, their long hair neatly tucked into buns, and began making their way, single file, down the dock behind the high priest, who led his entourage with the same gliding grace he had shown on stage. Men dressed in silk robes and slippers were not exactly a common sight at the commercial fishing dock in Mount Sinai, and the procession turned heads immediately.

One of the lobstermen looked up from his work, did a double-take, and called over to his buddy. "Hey Frankie, check out these freakin' people!"

The students, for their part, were equally dumbfounded. These men lived on a mountaintop in rural China, and most of them had never even seen the ocean, let alone a working fishing dock. They stopped to stare at the lobstermen unloading their catch, fascinated by the totes of lobsters and the strange machinery of a world completely foreign to their own.

One of the lobstermen noticed the monks staring and didn't take kindly to it. "What's up with these outfits, fellas? Who the hell are you guys?"

The martial artists didn't speak English, so they just kept staring, which only riled him up more.

"What the hell are you doing staring at me?" he said to the priest, his voice climbing. The priest only spoke Chinese and had no idea what this angry man on the dock was saying to him. He just continued to gaze with a big, placid smile on his face, serene as always, taking in this strange new world with the quiet wonder of a man who had spent his life in contemplation.

"What, you're just going to stare at me and say nothing? You got a problem, buddy?"

My stomach dropped. I was standing on the deck of my boat, a good hundred feet away, and I could see this thing escalating fast. I stepped off onto the dock and started moving toward the confrontation as quickly as I could without running.

"Hold on. Hold on!" I yelled as I closed the distance. "Please, just hold on. Trust me, man, you do not want to fight these guys."

"Yeah, right. I'd like to see that," one of them snapped back. These were men who worked the water with their hands every day, and they weren't used to being told that someone was tougher than them.

"I'm serious," I said, getting between them now. "Trust me on this one. What do you say we just calm down and let me get them on my boat and out of your way. Let's just forget about all of this, OK?"

A few of the lobstermen offered some choice words under their breath, but thankfully, they decided to let it go and turned back to their catch. I started shuffling my guests along the dock toward the boat, trying to move the whole procession as quickly and smoothly as I could. "Come on, guys. Let's go. Everyone, please just head straight to my boat. We don't want any problems here."

They boarded safely and sat quietly in their silk robes and slippers, smiling ear to ear, awaiting their big fishing adventure. My dad was already on the boat, and I saw him standing near the helm with a big grin on his face as the last of the monks settled in.

"That would not have been pretty, son. I think we almost just witnessed a homicide," he said. "Those fishermen had absolutely no idea what they were about to get themselves into."

We couldn't help but laugh. Disaster averted.

I turned my attention to my venerable guests. "Time to go fishing! You all ready for some fun?" I called out as I fired up the engine. "Let the dock lines go, Dad. We are off!"

As we made our way out of the harbor, I watched the high priest standing near the stern rail, taking in the open water with the same quiet stillness he carried everywhere. He was serene and completely at ease, though he also seemed somewhat reluctant to show any excitement. He appeared to live in that rare, placid, unflappable state of mindful presence, the kind that can only be cultivated through a lifetime of spiritual discipline and practice. No matter what I said to him through his translator, his only response was a gentle smile and a slight nod, never once breaking the role he embodied as the high priest of monastic splendor.

"Goodness, I've never met somebody so serene in all my life," I said to Dad on the way out.

All of that changed once we finally dropped our lines in the water.

I showed the priest how to hold the rod, turn the reel handle, bait his hook, and help him slowly lower his rig to the bottom. The bait had barely touched down when I saw the tip of his rod start to bounce as a hungry fish attacked from below.

"Set the hook! Reel! Reel!" I shouted. The priest looked at me, wide-eyed, not knowing what to do. "You got him! Reel! Turn the handle!" I lifted the rod to set the hook for him, and the rod doubled over with the weight of a good fish.

The priest began to crank the handle, turning it with all his might, and then something magical happened.

The unflappable, placid high priest of a Chinese martial arts monastery transformed right before our eyes. The serene master who carried himself with the composed stillness of a man beyond the reach of ordinary excitement was suddenly gone. In his place stood what I can only describe as a jubilant child, yelling and laughing with the kind of pure, unguarded glee that most of us leave behind somewhere around the age of five. He was jumping up and down on the deck, shaking his arms in the air, belly laughing in a way that I would not have believed was possible from the man I had watched glide across a stage just hours before.

He swung the fish over the rail, and I grabbed it for him. A beautiful big porgy, a good two pounds, its silver scales shimmering in the afternoon light. I held it up and asked him, through his translator, if he would like to touch his very first fish.

The priest considered this for a moment, then apprehensively agreed. He stretched out his pointer finger toward the porgy's head the way a three-year-old might reach toward something wondrous and slightly terrifying at the same time, his hand trembling just a little as it moved closer.

"Don't worry, he won't hurt you," I said gently. "You can touch him."

He mustered his courage, and the tip of his finger made contact with the fish. He squealed, pulled his hand back, shook it in the air, and then erupted into laughter so full and contagious that everyone on the boat joined in, my dad included. This man, who could leap through the air, wielding a sword with deadly precision, who commanded the respect of an entire monastery, who carried himself with the quiet authority of someone who had mastered both body and mind, was squealing like a little kid because he'd just touched a fish for the first time in his life.

When the laughter had settled, the high priest looked at me and began speaking through his translator.

"He wishes to tell you thank you. This moment has made him deeply happy."

Our eyes connected, and for a brief moment, something passed between us that needed no translation at all. We gave each other a gentle nod of respect, two men from completely different worlds who understood each other perfectly in that small, shared silence.

"Congrats on your first fish," I said. "Come on, you want to catch another one?"

His face lit up like a boy on Christmas morning. "Yes! Yes!" he said.

I baited his hook and helped him get back to the bottom, and he proceeded to catch another fish, and then another, and then another, laughing in playful bliss each time as though the joy of it never diminished, not even a little. His students lined up along the rail and started catching fish too, all of them transformed in the same way, their monastic composure dissolving into something much older and much more human. That joyful scene continued for the next hour until it was time to head for home.

As we made our way back into the harbor, I stood next to my dad in the wheelhouse and watched the monks sitting along the stern, still smiling, still glowing from the afternoon.

"That was something, Dad. Have you ever seen someone get so happy?"

"That was beautiful, son. What a great experience these men had. Certainly a day they won't soon forget."

We brought them safely back to the dock, Mom smiling all the way, completely unfazed by the day's adventures because this was simply how her life worked. Magic followed her, or maybe she followed it, and the rest of us were just lucky enough to be along for the ride.

The monks thanked us and said goodbye, and the next day they packed up and continued their tour across the country, promoting their martial arts and monastery.

After everyone had left and the boat was tied up and quiet, Dad and I stood on the dock for a moment, just the two of us. He looked at me with that familiar grin and shook his head slowly.

"Just another day in the life with my wife, Kathy O'Sullivan," he said.

I laughed and put my arm around him, and we walked up the dock together.

Halfway up, he stopped and looked back at the boat for a moment, then back at me.

"You've got a good thing going here, son," he said quietly. And that was all he needed to say. I knew exactly what he meant.

30

TWO CALLINGS

Business continued to grow over the next season. Word continued to spread throughout the fishing community, and the phone that used to sit idle for days was now starting to ring more than I could even answer.

By the following season, I was turning customers away on days I never expected to be full. It became a common refrain, one I heard almost daily:

"Damn, Cap, I've been trying to get on your boat for weeks, and you're always sold out. You gotta get a bigger boat."

They said it lovingly, laughing, but beneath the joke was something that still amazed me. Word had traveled through fishing circles up and down the island—if you wanted to get on the Celtic Quest, you'd better call well in advance and reserve your spot.

After a few seasons of this, I finally decided it was time to take the leap and look for a larger boat. My dad offered to come with me, and that winter we traveled up and down the coast together, searching marinas and boatyards from Montauk to the Jersey Shore.

Those long drives gave us time to talk in a way we rarely did at home. There's something about being in a car together, watching the miles pass, that loosens conversation. My dad loved to talk about his years in the fire service—the characters he worked with, the runs that stayed with him, the brotherhood of the firehouse. Even after his injury forced him out of the city, he'd stayed active as a chief in our local volunteer department. The fire service was in his blood.

"You know," he said on one of those drives, "a lot of the guys I came on the job with at the firehouse ran side businesses. Landscaping, contracting, and fishing charters. The schedule's perfect for it. What do you think about becoming a firefighter, possibly one day?

My dad had always dreamed that maybe one of his boys would someday become a New York City firefighter. I'd grown up in the firehouse, surrounded by that world, and part of me had always imagined following in his footsteps. Though I loved fishing with all my heart, since I was a young boy, there was a part of me that dreamed that one day I might be able to be a fireman too, just like my dad. I often contemplated how I might combine both callings. After all, solid pay and a pension might bring some stability, given how unpredictable fishing can be, and the idea of fighting fires genuinely excited me. With that, I had put my name on the New York City Fire Department list several years prior, just to keep my options open.

"Well, Dad," I said, "my name has been on the FDNY list for several years now— You never know, right?"

He glanced over at me.

"Obviously, I love fishing," I continued, "but it'd be amazing to be a fireman too, just like you and grandpa were. I could see myself doing both."

He smiled.

"But you know how hard it is to get called," I added. "I haven't heard anything in years." I kept my eyes on the road. "At this point, I don't think it's going to happen. And honestly, Dad, the business is doing well enough now that I think it's time to stop waiting. Time to go all in on fishing."

He nodded slowly—the way he always did when he was thinking something through—and we drove on in comfortable silence.

We looked at a lot of boats that winter. Some were too small. Some are too beaten down. Some were priced far beyond what I could manage. And then, one afternoon, we found her.

She sat in a marina on the south shore of Long Island—beautifully maintained, twice the size of my old boat, with twin diesels, a real cabin, and a proper wheelhouse. Her paint gleamed in the light, and you could tell immediately that her owner had taken pride in her over the years. She was nothing like the original Celtic Quest, which had been battered by years of neglect when I bought her.

This boat looked ready to work.

My dad and I stood on the dock, just staring.

"Wow," he said quietly. "Now *that* would be some boat for you, Des."

I tracked down the owner, and as fate would have it, he was looking to sell and upgrade to a larger vessel for his own business. Within days, we agreed on terms. I went to the bank, took out a mortgage, put everything I had into it—and just like that, the Celtic Quest II was in service.

She was more seaworthy and more comfortable than many boats I'd captained, and she could carry double the passengers. Some of my longtime customers teased me about the rustic conditions they'd endured on the first boat.

I remember Bobby—one of my very first customers who was with me that notorious day sinking in the dinghy with Capt Neil—stepping aboard the new boat for the first time.

"You mean we don't have to freeze our ass off and almost sink every trip?" he said, grinning.

I laughed. "Nope. We've even got cabin heat. And a toilet that actually works."

"Happy for you, Des," he said. "You've really come a long way since that first day sinking the dinghy with Captain Neil."

It felt good to share that moment with him. He knew as well as anyone how humble those beginnings had been.

This boat had separate men's and women's heads, both spotless, with running fresh water. The hull was tight and solid. The anchoring system was first-rate. Standing at the helm of such a vessel, I felt like I'd finally arrived at the place I'd been working toward all those years.

But no one appreciated the new boat more than my crew—the guys who had struggled alongside me through those early seasons. Especially my main crew member, Captain Chris.

Chris was one of my first hires and had worked tirelessly for me since the day he arrived. He worked his way up to being a trusted Captain, running the boat for me, let alone handling so much of the daily operations and maintenance. Never late once in all his years working for me, Chris truly treated my business like his own. He had kept the bilge pumps running on rough days, unclogged the rickety old toilet that barely worked, and hoped right along with me that the old girl would hold together as we pounded through the seas.

When we stepped aboard the Celtic Quest II together for the first time, our grins stretched ear to ear.

"Congrats, Des," Chris said, looking around the cabin. "And here's to us." He laughed and shook his head. "I'm just happy we survived Celtic Quest One."

I had gone all in. Taken out the mortgage. Invested everything. Doubled down on the dream I'd been chasing since I was a boy. The business was thriving, the boat was beautiful, and for the first time, I felt like I could stop holding my breath and trust that this was really going to work.

Fishing on our new boat felt like a dream come true. The customers loved it. The crew loved it. Everything was going so well. But then, about a month after we put the Celtic Quest II to work, a letter arrived in the mail.

I picked it up slowly from the counter, immediately noticing the New York City seal stamped on the envelope. My heart skipped as I opened it.

There it was.

"Congratulations. You have been appointed to the New York City Fire Department."

I folded the letter and set it back down. Outside, the harbor was quiet, the boats rocking gently in their slips. For years, I had imagined this moment, convinced that when it came, the answer would be obvious.

Instead, I felt the pull of two lives—both honorable, both demanding, both asking for everything I had.

And I knew that no matter what I chose next, something I loved would be left behind.

31

THE ROCK

I PUT THE LETTER IN THE NIGHTSTAND NEXT TO MY BED AND TRIED TO GET some rest. The next morning, I went for a long walk to gather my thoughts.

So many members of my family had built wonderful careers as cops and firemen. There was a part of me that felt called to follow that same path, even if it meant juggling two demanding lives. After all, the FDNY was a solid job with a pension, a brotherhood I understood, a calling that felt true to something deep inside me.

With all of that weighing on me, I responded to the letter and accepted my appointment.

I reported for duty the following week and drove into the city to the Probationary Firefighter School on Randall's Island, affectionately known by firefighters as "The Rock."

I did my best to fly under the radar, but the academy didn't let anyone escape. It was run by firefighters—many of them retired Marines—who took pride in breaking us down. Their mission was simple: weed out the weak.

Punishment was constant and creative. A loose helmet strap. A missed "sir." A half-second too slow. Drop. Push-ups. Arms shaking, sweat dripping onto the concrete. Day after day, they found reasons.

My demise came when they told us to shave our heads. I went home, buzzed everything off, and showed up the next morning thinking I was good to go. The meanest instructor walked the line, passed me once, then spun around and got right in my face.

"O'Sullivan," he said, hot breath on my ear. "You got some set on you, showing up here with that long hippie haircut."

He wrote my name down. From that day on, he made sure I earned it.

The real test came when they filled one of the buildings with smoke and sent us crawling inside. Visibility was zero. We moved on hands and knees until they ordered us to stand, remove our masks, and breathe.

The smoke hit like fire. Eyes burning. Lungs screaming. They made us sing "Happy Birthday" just to be sure we took it all in. Some guys panicked. A few quit on the spot.

If the smoke didn't get you, the ladder did. Four stories up, then over the side on a rope. I leaned back, heart pounding, trusting the line and forcing myself not to look down.

I made it through.

But driving home afterward—body wrecked, stuck in traffic, staring at brake lights for hours—I felt something else creeping in. Not fear. Not doubt.

Just a wondering.

That this life, this grind, might not be where I was meant to stay.

Graduation day finally arrived.

Standing in the ranks of the FDNY alongside my fellow probationary firefighters, I watched as each name was called and each graduate walked across the stage to shake hands with the Chief of Department and receive their badge. When my turn came, I stepped forward and felt the badge placed in my hand for the first time.

There was something electric in that moment—something powerful I couldn't quite name.

I looked over to where my dad was sitting in the crowd and saw the pride on his face, an expression I will never forget.

I was now a proud member of the New York City Fire Department.

32

TRAGEDY IN THE BRONX

After the ceremony, they posted our firehouse assignments. One of the other probationary firefighters was Mike Reilly—a great kid, steady and sharp, recently back from serving overseas. We'd battled through those hard months together, and when I saw both our names beside the same house—Ladder 33, Engine 75, Bronx—I felt a rush of relief. At least I wouldn't be walking into that place alone.

Mike and I stepped through the firehouse door on our first day like two deer in headlights. We did what probies do—we tried to be useful without getting in anyone's way. Dishes done. Coffee hot. Floors swept. Tools were wiped down on the apparatus floor until the metal shone. We moved fast and spoke little, watching the senior men out of the corners of our eyes, trying to read the room and figure out what kind of firefighters they expected us to become.

For the next month, I got a taste of the life: the banter, the adrenaline, the strange quiet between calls, the sound of the tones dropping in the middle of the night, and the sudden scramble toward the rigs. I loved the brotherhood. I loved what the job stood for. In so many ways, it was exactly what I thought I wanted.

But something wasn't right.

Balancing two lives—two jobs, two worlds—was starting to crush me. I'd watch my fishing boats push off into the sunrise with another hired Captain at the helm, gulls circling over the harbor, and then I'd get in my car and drive for hours into the city, crawling through rush-hour traffic while the day slipped away.

Back and forth I went, day after day, staring at brake lights, hearing a voice in the back of my mind that grew louder each week.

Maybe you're not meant to do this, Des. You're not meant to be a firefighter.

At first, I fought it. This was the job people dreamed of. A pension. Pride. Tradition. My family name stitched onto the uniform. So I kept forcing myself through it—kept showing up, kept telling myself to be grateful, kept pretending that grit would eventually make the feeling go away.

It didn't.

A few days later, I was taking out the trash, trying to be a good proby, when someone's broken glass sliced through the bag and into my knee. Blood soaked through my pant leg before I even made it to the can. I needed stitches and was put on sick leave.

A week away from the grind should have felt like relief. Instead, it felt like silence—real silence—the kind that finally lets you hear what you've been avoiding.

I spent that week on my boats. I worked. I laughed with customers. I watched the harbor change colors as the day turned. My nerves settled. Something simple and true returned to my chest.

On my last day off, I took my regulars out jigging for bluefish and bass. It was a great trip, and on the ride home, the wind dropped out completely. The water went glassy. Not a ripple. The sun slid down in the west and poured gold across the sound.

Standing at the helm in that stillness, I let myself imagine a life spent mostly in traffic—hours and hours sealed inside a car—while the boats I loved went out without me. The thought felt so heavy it was almost physical, like someone had laid a wet blanket across my shoulders. Something had to give.

That night, I prayed again—not eloquently, not bravely—just honestly.

God... please show me where I'm meant to be.

I tossed and turned all night, agonizing over one of the hardest decisions of my life.

The next morning, I woke with a thought so clear it felt like it didn't even come from me. Finally, from somewhere deep in my heart, the answer came.

I have to resign.

I put on my uniform, grabbed my coat and keys, and headed downstairs. The smell of fresh coffee drifted through the house—Dad had already brewed a pot. I knew he was awake somewhere, but I couldn't face him. Not yet. I slipped out the door like a kid sneaking back in after curfew and drove toward headquarters with my hands locked on the wheel.

I almost turned around twice, but continued on.

At headquarters, I stood outside the building for a long moment, looking up at it like it might speak first. Then I took a breath and walked in. HR led me to the Assistant Chief, who motioned for me to sit.

"What can I do for you, son?"

I dug deep and forced the words out.

"Chief… I'm here to hand in my badge. I'm resigning."

He stared at me. "You're resigning? After everything you just did to get here?"

"Sir… please don't make this harder than it already is. My mind is made up."

He studied me for a second. "You okay, son?"

"Honestly? I'm not sure."

I reached into my jacket and felt the cool metal one last time. Then I set the badge on his desk. The sound it made against the wood was small and final—like a door closing.

He looked down at it, then back up at me. For a moment, he didn't move, as if giving me one last chance to pick it back up.

"You sure?" he asked quietly.

I nodded. "Yes, sir."

He covered the badge with his hand. His face shifted—confusion giving way to something closer to resignation, like he'd seen this before. A young man trying to force himself into a life that wouldn't fit.

I stood up before I could change my mind.

The hallway felt longer on the way out. The elevator doors closed, and I was alone with the hum of the building. Somewhere between floors, the tears came. I didn't try to stop them.

What the hell did I just do?

I stepped out into the afternoon light and sat in my car for a moment, hands on the steering wheel, trying to breathe. And then the dread settled in—the ride home, the conversation with my dad waiting for me when I got home.

Mom met me at the door with that look only mothers have.

"Des... what are you doing home so soon? Are you okay?"

"Is Dad here?"

"He's in the kitchen."

He was sitting at the table, fresh from the garden, dirt still on his hands. I stood there a beat too long, then forced myself to speak.

"Dad... I have to tell you something."

He looked up.

I stared at the floor. "I... resigned. I handed in my badge today."

For a moment, he didn't say anything, like his mind couldn't catch up to the words.

"You what?" he finally said.

"I don't know why, Dad. I just... I'm miserable. I'm confused. I'm sorry."

His face changed—not with anger, not with disbelief—just with concern. He pushed his chair back and stood.

"Are you okay, son?"

"I... I don't know."

He shook his head slowly, as if trying to understand a language he didn't speak. He just stood there for a few moments, trying to comprehend what had just happened. Then, as he walked past me, he put a hand on my shoulder and gave it a gentle squeeze—one small gesture that carried everything he couldn't say. He was in disbelief, and I knew he just needed time to make sense of it all.

The next few days, my phone rang nonstop. Friends. Family. Firefighters. Everyone trying to talk sense into me. It was exhausting having to explain myself to everyone.

Finally, I just needed a break. I went upstairs, sat at my computer, and started scrolling without really seeing anything—just trying to quiet my mind.

Then I saw the headline.

BREAKING NEWS: Fatal Fire in the Bronx. Two Firefighters Killed.

My hand froze on the mouse.

Bronx. My company was in the Bronx.

I leaned closer, heart pounding, and there it was—a photograph beneath the story. Dress blues. Clean-shaven. That familiar, steady gaze.

Mike Reilly.

The room tilted. My chair scraped the floor as I pushed back too hard.

"No... no... no..."

The caption said the floor had given way at the fire scene. It said they'd fallen into the basement and they couldn't reach them in time.

"Des?" My father's voice came from the other room, alarm in it. "Everything okay?"

I couldn't answer. I just stared at the screen—at Mike's face, at the smoke rising behind the reporter in the video that had begun to play.

Dad appeared in the doorway. I pointed at the screen, unable to form words.

He read the headline. He looked at the photo. And then I watched the color drain from his face as he understood.

"Son," he said quietly, almost to himself, "that was supposed to be your next tour."

I nodded. I couldn't speak.

"You would have been there."

He crossed the room and put his hand on my shoulder, and we stood there together in the glow of the screen, watching smoke rise from a building I would have been inside. That could have been me they were carrying out of that building.

33

SPARED

In the days that followed, we attended Mike Reilly's memorial service. Thousands of firefighters lined the streets in their dress blues, and the bagpipes played as they carried him to rest. I stood among them wearing civilian clothes now, feeling conspicuous and strange—like a man who had stepped out of a photograph he no longer belonged in. The sound of those pipes cut right through me. I watched the flag-draped casket pass and thought of Mike clearing the table beside me in the firehouse kitchen, both of us just trying to make a good impression, both of us with no idea what lay ahead.

It all felt overwhelming. The randomness of it. The sadness. The timing. The fact that I had walked away from that job only days before the floor gave way beneath the men who took my place.

My dad was struggling with it too. His mind kept circling what might have been, what almost was. But this wasn't the first tragedy he had lived through as a fireman, and with that came a wisdom that steadied him—and, in turn, steadied me.

On the drive home from the funeral, my dad turned to me with a look I hadn't seen before. It wasn't disappointment anymore. There was no doubt anymore. It was something closer to acceptance.

"Son," he said, "I'm so glad you chose to follow your heart."

I didn't say anything. I just listened.

"Had I pushed you—had I tried to talk you out of it—and then something happened to you at that fire..." He paused and shook his head slowly. "I don't know if I could have lived with myself. The guilt would have been unbearable."

He looked at me for a long moment.

"Just thank God it all worked out," he said. "Your angels knew where you needed to be, and they protected you."

My dad was a faithful man—a church-going Catholic who believed God worked in mysterious ways. He had spent his entire career in the fire service and once wanted nothing more than to see his son follow in his footsteps. But now he understood what I had been too confused to articulate. Sometimes you have to trust that the voice inside you knows something your mind does not.

It took a few weeks to absorb what had happened—to sit with the enormity of it, to let the truth of it settle into my body. I thought constantly about poor Mike Reilly, his grieving family, and all the other brave firefighters who were killed or injured on that terrible day. How easily that could have been me instead of them.

I had followed my heart against every voice of reason, and that choice had spared my life. There was no way to explain it except as grace—as guidance, as the hand of God—steering me toward where I was always meant to go.

And with that understanding came a kind of peace I had never known before. The wrestling was over. The questioning was over. I knew now that my path was the water—that it had always been the water—and that every detour and delay had simply been preparing me for this moment.

I knew exactly what I was meant to do with my life, and I was ready to pour everything I had into doing it. The Celtic Quest was waiting—and so were the customers I hadn't met yet, the crew I hadn't hired yet, the fleet I hadn't built yet.

It was time to get to work.

34

THOUSANDS OF SMILES

WITH NEWFOUND CLARITY, I FELT A NEW VIGOR IN MY STEP AND QUIET excitement for the future. My father threw his full support behind me, too. He ran errands, picked up supplies, and helped me with whatever needed doing. At the end of each day, he would come down to the boat to help me reconcile the books or tidy up the dock. He wasn't just supportive from a distance. He was in it with me.

Business grew even faster now.

We served everyone. Corporations came out for team-building trips. Boy Scout troops and Girl Scout troops earned badges on our decks. Schools sent busloads of kids who had never held a fishing rod, and we put rods in their hands and taught them how to feel the joy of catching their first fish. School trips and summer camps became a staple—sometimes a hundred kids a day, pouring onto the boats with the kind of energy that lit up the deck with joyful laughter.

What had once been a small operation grew into something I never could have imagined back in those early days in Mount Sinai, when Celtic Quest was all I had and all I needed. After the second boat came Celtic Quest III, a smaller charter vessel, and then eventually the two big ones—Celtic Quest IV and Celtic Grace—each capable of carrying over a hundred passengers in comfort. Standing on the dock some mornings, looking out at that fleet, I had to remind myself that this was real—that this was mine—that this was my life now.

The business had become something I could no longer run alone. Dozens of people came to work for me, and many of them stayed. Some stayed for years and are still with us to this day. They raised their families on this work. They paid their mortgages, put their kids through school, and devoted themselves to this business the way I had. I never took that lightly. A fishing boat is only as good as the crew that runs it, and I was blessed with people who cared as much as I did.

My father fell in love with the business too, and it meant everything to have him by my side. He had a favorite bench down by the water, right near the boats, facing the inlet. From there, he could watch the fleet set sail each day. He loved nothing more than sitting on that bench, watching the operation hum along. He'd chat with customers as they came and went, but mostly he just sat there, taking in what had grown.

One afternoon, I came in from a trip and walked over to keep him company. It was a warm July day, and he was soaking up the sun, sipping a cold soda. A camp group was loading up for the next run. A hundred kids climbed aboard, laughing and shouting, while dozens of parents stood on the dock waving, phones held high to capture the moment. The boat backed out of the slip, kids screaming with joy, and my father watched it all in silence for a long moment.

Then he turned to me and said, "You know, you're gonna make a lot of kids really happy today."

I didn't say anything. I just sat there with him and watched the boat head out toward the Sound. He was right. And somehow—without ever planning it, without ever knowing how it would all play out—this had become my life.

Making people happy. Thousands of people a year. Season after season.

I felt like the luckiest man in the world.

35

THE SWEETEST MOMENTS

"MAN, THAT IS SOME FISH, RICHIE!"

I grabbed the net and moved toward the starboard stern, where he was fighting to keep his rod tip up. The fluke broke the surface, and I knew before I brought the net up that this was the one he'd been chasing for years—a summer flounder pushing double digits, broad as a dinner platter, that unmistakable olive-brown shimmering in the June sun.

I lifted the net over the gunwale, and Richie started screaming, high-fiving everyone within reach, his whole face lit up like a kid on Christmas morning.

"You finally did it, man! You finally caught the double-digit trophy you've been talking about for years!"

"Thank you, Captain! You have no idea how hard I've tried to catch one like this!"

"Giant fish and happiness, Richie, that's what we are all about!"

He laughed. "Well, you certainly delivered on that today, cap!"

It was the kind of June day that reminds you why you do this work—air warm, sun pouring down, the water still carrying that spring coolness that keeps it calm as a lake. And here was Richie, a man who had fished with us nearly every week for years, finally holding the fish of his dreams.

Richie was the best. He showed up week after week, always with that same easy laugh, always making the boat a little lighter just by being aboard. He had a way of arriving with an egg sandwich for me in the morning or cookies from the local bakery tucked under his arm, never asking if I wanted them—just handing them over like it was the most natural thing in the world. That was the kind of soul he was. Generous without ceremony.

So when two weeks passed, and Richie didn't show, I knew something was wrong. He never missed fluke season. Not once.

Then one of his buddies pulled me aside on the dock and told me. Richie had been diagnosed with cancer.

Terminal.

The news hit me like a rogue wave—the kind that comes out of nowhere and knocks you off your feet. Just a few weeks earlier, he had been jumping up and down on my deck, celebrating the catch of his life. He had never let on that anything was wrong. Not a word about the symptoms he must have already been feeling, the tests, the waiting. He just showed up, fished, and laughed like he always did.

Richie began treatment right away. Chemotherapy—the brutal kind that takes everything out of you in the hope of taking the disease with it. He fought hard for several months, but despite his will to live, the cancer was winning. I did my best to support him, to cheer him on when we talked, but I could feel his strength beginning to fade.

Eventually, he was admitted to hospice care, where they did what they could to manage his pain and allow for a gentle passage.

Knowing that he was nearing the end of his life, I went to visit him. I walked into his room on a quiet afternoon. The lights were dim, and the only sound was the steady beeping of the monitors he was hooked to. His wife sat quietly at his bedside, holding his hand. She looked up when she saw me in the doorway.

"Des, I'm so glad you're here. Please, come in."

I sat down beside him and took his hand in mine. It was cold, the fingers thin and frail— nothing like the strong grip I remembered from all those days on the boat.

"He's been unconscious for three days now," his wife said. Her face carried the look of someone who had been through a terrible battle and was nearing its end. The grief hung heavy in that room, but so did a kind of exhausted relief. This awful fight was almost over. Soon, he could rest.

We sat together in silence for a while, speaking softly to him now and then, telling him we loved him, that it was okay to let go. Once in a while, I felt the faintest squeeze of his hand.

Then Richie began to stir.

He opened his eyes for the first time in days, scanning the dim room, orienting himself. His gaze found his wife first—that familiar face of love and reassurance—and he took a breath. Then he turned his head and saw me sitting there beside him.

A smile broke across his face. He squeezed my hand.

He closed his eyes and took a few slow breaths, and I thought he might drift off again. But then he opened them once more, and this time the smile grew even brighter. He let go of my hand and raised his arms from the bed, lifting them maybe a foot off the mattress, and began making the motion of setting a hook. Then he moved one hand in that familiar circular motion—reeling in a fish only he could feel.

This was a man who had barely moved in days. And yet he found the strength to show me he was fishing one last time.

He looked at me, still smiling, and a silence passed between us. But I knew exactly what he was saying.

There was nothing sweeter than those simple moments on the water. In the final hours of his life, with everything else falling away, this is what remained. This is what mattered. And in his own quiet way, he was thanking me for the way our lives had crossed as fishermen.

He closed his eyes and drifted back to sleep. I sat for a while longer holding his hand and then slowly stepped away.

Richie died peacefully a few hours later, his wife at his side. Finally, his hard journey had come to an end.

I still keep a picture of him on my computer, holding that giant fluke from that June morning when everything was still good. No matter what kind of day I'm having, it makes me smile. I can hear his laugh as if it were yesterday.

Sometimes, in moments when I wonder if what I do matters as much as some other profession, I think about Richie in that hospice bed—raising his arms to set the hook one last time.

And I remember that when our time comes, it won't be the titles or the status or the money we reach for—it will be the moments that quietly shaped us, long before we ever knew how much they mattered.

36

YEARNING

RICHIE'S DEATH STAYED WITH ME FOR A LONG TIME. NOT AS GRIEF, exactly, but as a kind of clarity. He had reminded me of something I already knew but needed to see again—that in the end, it's the people we love and the moments we share with them that matter most. Everything else falls away.

And maybe that's why, in the months that followed, I became more aware of what was still missing in my own life.

The business was thriving. I had built something I was proud of—something that brought joy to thousands of people every season. I had a great family, a beautiful condo, and financial security earned through years of hard work. By any measure, I was blessed beyond what I ever could have imagined back in those early days when I was terrified about making payroll.

But at the end of a long day on the water, my crew went home to their wives and children.

And I went home to an empty condo, alone.

Late nights were the hardest. Sitting at the kitchen counter, the boat was finally quiet for the day, eating dinner off a paper plate and realizing there was no one to tell about the small wins—the things that only mattered to me.

So many Valentine's Days passed without anyone to share them with. Birthdays could sting a little too—watching friends have parties thrown for them by their spouses, surrounded by the families they had built. My parents always did their best to help me celebrate, and I was grateful for that. But it wasn't the same thing.

I had met many women over the years, dated some for a time, and lived with one for a few years. Friends were constantly trying to set me up. But I never found that magical spark—that feeling of recognition and comfort you feel when you're finally with the right person. I began to wonder if maybe I just wasn't meant to find it.

So I prayed. Not for God to send me a wife, exactly, but for something deeper than that.

God, I trust you.

If it is your will for me to meet my wife in this life, then may my heart be open enough to hear that calling. And may you guide me each step of the way.

THAT WAS MY PRAYER.

Surrender. Trust.An open heart.

And then, I let go.

37

THE BEGINNING OF US

THE DRIVEWAY TO THE HEALTH CENTER I LOVED TO GO TO FROM TIME TO time curved through oak trees just starting to turn, their leaves catching the October light. I'd been a bit annoyed at myself for having left my bag there the day before—but by the time I parked, something about the old Victorian house they had turned into a health center, with its gardens and wide windows, had already begun to soften my mood.

Inside, the lobby smelled of lavender and eucalyptus, and Liquid Mind played softly through hidden speakers—that slow orchestral drift that makes you breathe deeper whether you mean to or not. I looked around for my belongings and noticed a well-dressed woman with a kind face sitting across the room. She smiled, and we fell into easy small talk about the day, the weather, and the beauty of the property in autumn.

Judith, the center's owner, walked in a moment later. "Des! So glad you're here. You have to meet my friend Michele—she's been a dear friend for many years."

"We were just chatting," I said. "Nice to meet you formally, Michele."

We exchanged a few more words before Judith apologized and

explained she was on a tight schedule. She and Michele disappeared into her office and closed the door. I didn't think much of the encounter beyond the fact that Michele seemed genuinely warm and kind. I gathered my bag from where I'd left it by the window and started toward the door.

I stopped at the front desk to say hello to the office manager, someone I'd gotten to know over my visits. We were mid-conversation when the lights flickered hard, and the entire computer system went dark.

"Oh my goodness," she said, staring at the blank screen. "The whole system just crashed. I have no idea how to fix this." She stood up, looking panicked. "I hate to do this, but I need to pull Judith out of her session."

She knocked lightly on the office door, and a moment later Judith emerged, apologizing to Michele for the interruption. She took a seat behind the desk and began rebooting the system while the office manager hovered nearby.

I watched them troubleshoot for a minute, not sure whether to stay or go. Then I turned around and found Michele standing beside me, looking like she wanted to speak.

She pressed her hand to her heart. "Listen," she said, her voice a little unsteady. "I'm so sorry if I'm out of line. I never do this." She looked almost embarrassed, but something in her eyes told me she wasn't going to stop herself. "The whole time I was sitting in there waiting for Judith, I couldn't help thinking about coming out here to ask you something."

I was surprised—and a little amused by her shyness. "Sure, Michele. What is it?"

She took a breath. "By any chance... are you single?"

I laughed softly. "Why yes, actually. I am."

She exhaled like she'd been holding her breath. "You are?" she said, suddenly animated. "From the moment we started talking, I just kept thinking you'd be perfect for my best friend, Carin. Would you be open to meeting her?"

My heart fluttered. "Tell me about her," I said.

"She's just the best person. Super spiritual, loves the water, teaches meditation. I really think you two would hit it off." Michele was already pulling out her phone. "Let me show you a picture."

She turned the screen toward me, and I saw a beautiful woman standing in a wide green field surrounded by children. Hundreds of them—it looked like five hundred kids sitting on the grass at a school —and Carin was leading them all in meditation. Her face was calm, focused, and kind.

I stared at the image for a long moment. What kind of person, I thought, can hold the attention of five hundred children in stillness?

"I'd love to meet her," I said. "Give her my number."

Michele's face broke into a huge smile. "Really? Oh, I'm so excited!" She typed my number into her phone, and then Judith called her back in to finish their session.

I walked out into the October afternoon. It felt like something had shifted. I didn't yet know what any of it meant, but I felt it in my chest —something electric—and I knew this meeting was something special.

Michele later told me she could barely focus for the rest of her session. The moment she got to her car, she called Carin.

"Carin," she said, "I just met your husband."

Carin had been through her own long road of relationships and setups that went nowhere. She was skeptical. "Come on, Michele. Do I really have to go on another date?"

"If you don't call this guy," Michele said, "I swear we're not going to be friends anymore."

She was half-kidding.

But only half.

A forgotten bag. A computer crash. A few minutes of small talk in a sunlit lobby.

That's all it took.

That's how close I came to walking out the door and never knowing that I was about to meet the woman of my dreams.

38

MAGIC IN THE AIR

I PULLED MY TRUCK INTO THE DRIVEWAY AT CARIN'S HOME ON THE SOUTH shore, and before I even stepped out, I could see her walking toward me. She had beautiful, long blonde hair and a smile that radiated kindness. We met on the pavement, both of us carrying some jitters, I think, the kind that come when something feels like it might actually matter. But when we hugged, something settled.

Tula Kitchen was a quaint little vegetarian place not far from her house, the kind of restaurant where the food is beautifully prepared and fresh. We both loved healthy eating, so it seemed like a good choice. The hostess seated us in a booth near the back, and we slid in across from each other, menus in hand, but already talking before we'd even glanced at them.

The conversation came easily. We discovered we both grew up on the water—she'd spent her summers on the Great South Bay, sailing and swimming, and understood in her bones what it means to live where the land meets the sea. That shared language opened everything else. We talked about family, about faith, about the choices that had shaped our lives. The food came and went, plates of colorful vegetables we barely noticed because we were too busy listening, too deep in each other's stories to keep track of time.

At some point, the waitress came by to check on us—a middle-aged woman who moved with the confidence of someone who'd worked there for years. We mentioned, almost shyly, that this was our first date together.

Her face lit up. She leaned in close, like she was sharing a secret.

"You know," she said, "you're actually sitting at what we call our love booth."

Carin and I looked at each other.

"This is a big restaurant," the waitress continued, "but for some reason, this particular booth—right where you're sitting—is where I know for a fact multiple marriages have started. Something about the feng shui, maybe. But couples sit here on their first date and end up married."

We both blushed a little. There was a spark of something in that moment, a flutter of possibility neither of us wanted to name out loud.

I looked at Carin and smiled. "Hey, you never know."

The hours kept disappearing. She told me about Mission Be, the charity she'd started after the Sandy Hook shooting to teach children mindfulness and meditation. She'd been a social worker with a tenured position at the local high school—a job her family thought she was crazy to leave. But she did it anyway. She bought a plane ticket to California and started building something from nothing. By the time I met her, she'd reached thousands of students across the country.

Her story reminded me of my own. That same leap of faith. That same moment when everyone around you says you're out of your mind, and you do it anyway because something in your heart won't let you stay.

Then she told me about the beach.

A few days before I had met her friend at the health center, she'd gone to Fire Island. She walked along the sand for hours, bundled against the cool fall air, the waves crashing and seagulls skittering out of her path as she moved down the shoreline. She walked through the afternoon and into dusk, losing track of time, losing track of everything except the prayer rising up from somewhere deep inside.

She looked at me with a kind of quiet intensity when she described it.

"It wasn't just an ordinary prayer," she said. "It came from years of heartache. Years of choosing the wrong men. I finally just surrendered. I said, God, I give my will to you. Obviously, my choices haven't worked. So if it be your will, bring me an honest, kindhearted man. A strong spiritual man. And I'll trust wherever you lead me."

She told me how she'd walked for miles in that state of surrender, the light fading to pink and orange over the water, and how something felt different when she finally stopped. Like something had shifted.

The next night, her best friend Michele took her to dinner and gave her a pep talk. Michele had grabbed her hand and said, "Carin, I feel it. Your ship is coming in. You're going to meet the man you're praying for."

The day after that, I walked into a health center for an appointment I'd scheduled months ago.

But the story that stopped my heart came later in the evening, when the restaurant was getting ready to close and we'd long since lost track of how many times our waitress had refilled our water glasses.

Carin told me that for years, she'd had a sense—a feeling she couldn't explain—that her soulmate was a fisherman in Montauk. She didn't know when she would meet him. She didn't know how. But once a year, she would get in her car and drive all the way out to Montauk at the end of Long Island. There she would walk the docks, wondering if the love of her life was somewhere nearby.

And every time, she said, she felt called to stop at a local dive bar near the commercial fishing boats. A place called The Dock.

My whole body went still.

The Dock was where all the locals hung out—fishermen still in their boots and hooded sweatshirts, coming in after work to catch up on local drama and fishing reports. It was dark and unpretentious, the kind of place where nobody cared what you looked like as long as you knew how to tell a good story. Carin was much too pretty for a place like that. But something in her heart told her to go there anyway, year after year, looking for someone she hadn't met yet.

That was the same bar where my buddies and I ate lunch almost every day during my years in Montauk.

We might have passed each other a dozen times and never known it.

I sat there with chills running through me, trying to take in what she was telling me. All those years, something in her had known I was out there. Her heart had led her to the exact right place. We just hadn't been ready yet.

By the time we left, the staff was stacking chairs. I drove her home through the dark, and when I pulled into her driveway, neither of us moved to get out right away.

Then I hopped out to say goodbye. It had been a wonderful evening—one of those rare ones where time bends and hours feel like minutes.

I told her how much I truly enjoyed her company.

We hugged and held it for a few extra seconds, neither of us wanting to let go.

"Thank you," I said. "This was a really great night with you."

She smiled and put her hand on my cheek. She didn't say anything, but I knew she agreed.

39

WHEN IT JUST FEELS RIGHT

THE MONTHS AFTER THAT FIRST DATE UNFOLDED THE WAY GOOD THINGS DO when you stop trying to control them. Carin and I spent more and more time together, learning each other's rhythms, discovering how much we had in common, laughing at how long it had taken us to finally meet.

Her family welcomed me in like I'd always been there. She was one of seven children, and they were all still close, living on the south shore of Long Island. Her Mom, Mary Ellen, was the matriarch and reminded me of my own mother—an amazing caregiver with a huge heart, not to mention an incredible cook who loved to treat her family to glorious, delicious meals.

The first day I met them, she put out a feast, and the house was loud with conversation, cousins, and the kind of chaos that only big families know how to make. It felt familiar and inviting. Her father was a wonderful, hardworking, church-going man, much like my own dad, and I took to him immediately. There were so many shared values between our families that I felt right at home almost instantly.

After a few months, we decided to take a trip together. We flew to Puerto Rico and rented a condo in Rincón, a little place overlooking the water where you could hear the waves from our bedroom. Each morning we'd wake to that sound and make our way out to the balcony with coffee and tea, watching the light come up over the ocean while we talked about our lives—all the adventures and heartaches that had come before, all the roads that had somehow led us to our synchronous meeting.

One morning stands out above the rest. The sun was already warm, and a gentle breeze rolled in off the water, lifting the white curtains on the balcony doors. We decided to meditate together, something we'd started doing more and more. I closed my eyes and let the sound of the waves carry me inward.

What happened next is hard to put into words.

I felt the presence of our grandparents— long since passed—and there was a warmth that came with them, a sense of blessing. It wasn't a vision exactly, more like a knowing. A message about family, about love, about how nothing matters more than being good to the people in your life.

When we opened our eyes, Carin looked at me with tears in her eyes.

"Did you feel that?" she asked.

I nodded.

She told me what she'd experienced, and it was almost identical to mine—our grandparents, the same sense of blessing, the same message. We hadn't spoken a word during the meditation, hadn't known what the other was feeling. But somehow, we'd gone to the same place.

It felt like an anointing. Like the elders of both our families had come to say, *You two are meant to be together. Go have fun. Be good to each other. We love you.*

After that trip, moving in together wasn't even a question. We'd both been through enough relationships to know when something was different. I didn't feel the need to impress her or stay one step ahead of the moment. I just felt myself settle. And that was new. We threw caution to the wind and went for it.

My parents took to her immediately. They were older now, needing more help around the house—cooking, cleaning, rides to doctor's appointments. Carin jumped right in without being asked. She'd show up with groceries, sit and talk with my mother for hours, and treated them like they were her own. My parents constantly told me I was a lucky man to have found such a good woman.

I knew they were right. For the first time in a long time, I had a true partner by my side. Someone I could share the beauty of each day with. Someone I could laugh with and lean on. Someone who understood the spiritual path I was walking because she was walking it too.

Everything felt like it was finally falling into place.

PART IV

HEART OF THE GALE

40

SABOTAGE

I WAS SITTING AT MY DESK FINISHING UP PAPERWORK WHEN MY PHONE rang. Jared's voice told me something was wrong before he finished his first sentence.

"Des, I've got some really bad news."

"What is it?"

"Someone broke into your boat at the shipyard and destroyed your engine and transmission. Filled everything with saltwater, sand, and rocks. Once it circulated through, it was over."

For a moment, I couldn't speak. When the words finally landed, I put my head in my hands and slammed my fist on the desk.

"Who would do something like that? Why would anyone do this?"

"I don't know," he said quietly. "Nobody deserves this. But you need to get down here."

I called the police and drove straight to the marina. It was the dead of winter at Shellfish Marine, the yard quiet and nearly empty, boats sitting motionless on their blocks waiting for spring.

I climbed the ladder and stepped aboard, and the first thing I noticed was the silence. Shipyards are never quiet—there's always a grinder running somewhere, a compressor kicking on, somebody banging on something. But that morning, everything was still.

The engine room hatch was already open, a faint glow rising from below. I walked over and looked down, and my stomach turned.

Saltwater and antifreeze pooled on the floorboards, still glistening under the drop lights. The engine block was streaked with grit and residue, and when I climbed down the ladder and got close enough to see, I could make out sand and rocks scattered across the engine rack. There was no doubt—the engine was destroyed.

Jared was crouched by the transmission, his hands covered in oil, his face grim.

"I'm sorry, Des," he said quietly. "I've never seen anything like this."

I didn't answer. I kept looking at the engine, trying to make sense of it all. Standing there, I felt the unfairness of it settle in. Not rage. Just confusion.

I climbed back up onto the deck and sat down on the cold bench, peering out over the shipyard, my mind reeling.

The police took their statements, but the surveillance footage had been erased. Whoever did this had planned it carefully, and they were long gone.

I didn't know how I was going to fix it. All I knew was that standing there doing nothing wasn't an option—even if, for the first time, I wasn't sure how much fight I had left.

I took a breath and resigned myself to the fact that there was nothing left to do but get to work. We would have to cut the boat apart to lift the machinery with a crane out through the cabin and top deck—weeks of labor and tens of thousands of dollars, on top of the structural rebuild we were already working on.

Realizing we had no other choice, I grabbed the circular saw, unwrapped the cord, and walked to the area above the engine. And then I started cutting.

As the saw blade screamed through the ceiling and sawdust filled the cold air, it felt wrong to cut apart something we had poured so much care into. But we continued on.

The job was painfully slow. Even still, the crew showed up day after day. My captains, Chris and Mark, along with the rest of the guys, worked tirelessly—covered in fiberglass dust and oil, crawling through tight spaces, solving one problem after another. Sometimes I would stop and watch them—hands raw, faces tired—and feel a quiet gratitude settle over me.

There was one night, a few weeks into the rebuild, when I stayed at the yard long after everyone else had gone home. The drop lights flickered overhead, casting that cold industrial glow over everything, and I sat on an overturned bucket in the middle of the gutted cabin, surrounded by sawdust, tools, and the skeleton of what used to be my boat.

I was exhausted. Not just physically—though my back ached and my hands were cut up—but the kind of tired that settles into your bones and makes you wonder if you have anything left to give.

I called Carin.

"Hey," she said. "You still there?"

"Yeah." I looked around at the destruction. "I don't know how we're going to do this."

"You'll do it because you always do," she said, calm and steady. "One day at a time. One step at a time. That's how you built everything else."

I didn't say anything for a moment. I just listened to her voice on the other end of the line, and something in me settled.

"Come home soon, Des, and get some rest."

"Okay, love. I'll be there soon. I just have to finish a few things."

I hung up the phone and sat there a few minutes longer, looking at the mess around me. Even though everything in me wanted to quit, I knew that wasn't an option. So I stood up, grabbed my tools, and got back to work.

41

SALT IN THE WOUND

After several weeks of work, against all odds, the new engine was in. The cabin was whole again, the worst of the damage finally behind us. I gathered my crew together at the end of the day.

"I'm proud of every one of you," I told them. "I don't know how we pulled this off, but we did. Steak dinner's on me next week."

That night, for the first time in weeks, I went home feeling like I could finally breathe. A long hot shower, a real meal, and I sat down at the table, letting the tension drain from my body.

Then my phone rang.

Jared again. *Why would he be calling me now?*

My stomach dropped.

"Des, I hate to make this call. The engine we installed is no good. I've been working on it for hours—serious internal issues. There's no way it's safe to run."

I stood up so fast my chair fell backward. "That's impossible. The factory tested that engine."

"I know. It has major, major issues, and I hate to say this, but there's no saving it. We need to take it out of the boat."

I hung up the phone and just stood there, staring at nothing.

For a long moment, I couldn't move. The anger came first—a hot, surging wave that made me want to put my fist through the wall. We had just finished. We had just put the boat back together, piece by piece, after weeks of grinding labor. And now this.

Then the anger gave way to something heavier. I sank into the chair and put my head in my hands, and I felt the weight of it all pressing down on me—the sabotage, the rebuild, the money hemorrhaging out of my accounts, the season slipping away while my boat sat useless in the yard. My heart was pounding.

I thought about calling Carin, but I didn't know what I would say. I thought about calling my dad, but I didn't want him to hear the defeat in my voice.

So I just sat there in the dark, alone with my thoughts, until it became clear there was only one way forward from here.

Get up. Go back to the yard. Do it again.

That was the only thing we could do.

The next morning, when I gathered the crew and told them, Chris stared at me as if I were playing a sick joke.

"You've got to be freakin kidding me."

I shook my head.

He held my eyes for a long moment, then sat down heavily at one of the tables and put his head in his hands. Nobody spoke. I think they were waiting for me to change my mind or offer another alternative. Then they finally realized this was the path forward.

Chris took a breath, looked up, and stood.

"Well," he said, "I just don't even know what to say. But I guess it is what it is."

He walked to where we'd stored the tools, picked up the skill saw, and unwound the cord. I could hear him muttering as he plugged it in. When the blade bit into the wood we'd just finished installing, sawdust rising fresh into the air once again, it hurt worse than the first time. It was like nails on a chalkboard screeching through your body. Every one of us felt it.

Once again, the crew worked tirelessly, and weeks later, after cutting the boat apart a second time, craning out the machinery, installing a new engine, finishing all the carpentry, fiberglass, wiring, flooring, and painting, the boat was whole again.

When the engine finally turned over and ran clean, nobody cheered. We were too tired for that. But Chris caught my eye across the deck and gave me a single nod—the kind that says more than words ever could. We had done the impossible twice, and we had done it together.

We had missed the first few weeks of the season—other boats posting fishing reports while we were still buried in the yard, each one adding insult to injury.

When we finally got back on the water, I remember finally anchoring up on a warm spring day and standing alone on the top deck. Below me, the crew worked the customers, rods bending over the rail, laughter drifting up to the wheelhouse. The sun felt good on my face. I stood there looking out over the water and let out a long breath.

I was still shaking my head. I didn't understand why any of it had happened, and I knew by then that I never would. Some things aren't meant to be explained. You endure them, and eventually you surrender to the fact that they simply are. Sometimes, that is really all you can do.

42

WORDS YOU NEVER FORGET

Despite the late start, we managed to get right back into our season. The fishing that spring started off really strong, and thankfully, we were carrying well. However, one thing became very apparent. I was starting to struggle with my vision.

I finally reached the point where I could barely even read my phone or words on a page without squinting. I'd been telling myself it was stress from the engine issues, exhaustion, and the accumulated weight of so many seasons running boats. Carin had been after me for weeks to see someone, and I'd finally relented and made an appointment with an ophthalmologist.

He did a battery of tests, but something in his voice had shifted when he looked up from his instruments.

"Des, the good news is... your eyes look fine to me. But the bad news… I think there might be something going on behind your eyes," he'd said. "In your brain. I need to get you an MRI as soon as possible." I could tell he was concerned, and my whole body tensed. This was not the news I was expecting to hear.

I went straight for an MRI and then headed back to the Celtic Quest office. I was going over the schedule with my office staff, Bernadette and Susan, trying to focus on the work in front of me, when I saw my doctor's name on the caller ID a few hours later. My stomach dropped, and my heart started to race. Doctors don't call back the same day unless there's something to say.

I answered immediately. Bernadette and Susan had been working at their desks, but they turned to look at me now, and I could tell from their faces that something in my voice had changed.

"Des, I'm sorry." My doctor's tone was gentle in the way that prepares you for what comes next. "It's what we feared. You have a massive brain tumor—a huge one, right in the center of your brain. We don't know yet if it's malignant or benign, but this needs to be addressed immediately."

I heard myself asking questions, my voice sounding far away. How bad?

"Really bad, Des. You need to cancel everything else and focus solely on getting help."

When I hung up, I was doing my best to hold it together. But then I turned and saw Bernadette's face, tears already streaming down her cheeks, and something in me broke open. I just started crying.

Carin crossed the room and put her arms around me, holding me tight, and I felt her profound love and strength flowing into me as we stood there suspended in time, trying to understand what had just happened. This was the kind of moment you read about happening to other people, the kind of news that arrives in someone else's life. But here I was.

I had woken up that morning thinking about breakfast, about walking the dog, about the boats and the business, and now, hours later, I was standing in my own office learning that I might be dying.

All my worries about the fleet, about bookings and repairs and schedules, fell away as they had never mattered at all. What you think is a problem becomes almost laughable when you realize how quickly everything can change.

That night, I lay in bed unable to sleep, my mind racing through corridors I couldn't close off. You think about everything when death is staring you in the face—all the things you hoped to do, all the moments you assumed you'd have, all the ordinary days you never thought to treasure.

I found myself flashing back to Kenya, to that long night when a hippo circled my tent in the darkness and I lay still listening to its breathing, knowing that the canvas between us was nothing, that I was utterly at the mercy of forces beyond my control. The thoughts I had now felt eerily similar: the same helplessness, the same bargaining with whatever powers might be listening, the same fragile hope that dawn would come and I would still be here.

At some point, I got up and stood at the window, looking out at the night sky. The moon hung there, pale and indifferent, and I wondered if this might be one of the last times I would get to gaze upon it. If my diagnosis turned out to be terminal, how many more moons would I see? Five? Ten? The thought was almost too large to hold.

43

WAITING TO KNOW

THE NEXT MORNING, CARIN SPRANG INTO ACTION. WHILE I WAS STILL trying to process what was happening to me, she was already on the phone, working her contacts, refusing to wait for the slow machinery of referrals and appointments. By midday, she had managed to secure a consultation with one of the top neurosurgeons at NYU, and just like that, we were in the car heading into the city. The day before, I had been worrying about fishing schedules and boat repairs, and now I was riding shotgun while Carin drove because my vision had deteriorated to the point that I could no longer safely drive.

There was an intensity in the air between us, the kind of silence that holds too much to speak, so we put on some of our favorite music and let it fill the space. From time to time, Carin would glance over and squeeze my hand. "Everything's going to be okay, love," she would say, and I wanted so badly to believe her. Then we crossed the bridge into Manhattan, the energy of the city rising up around us, and made our way down to NYU Medical Center.

The place was overwhelming. A massive complex bustling with people shuffling in every direction—doctors in white coats striding past, patients being pushed along in gurneys, constant announcements crackling over the intercoms. At one point, I watched a nurse push a man about my age past us on a gurney, his head bandaged, his eyes half-closed, looking like he had just come through major surgery. A shiver ran down my spine as I realized that could be me within days.

The doctor's office, when we finally reached it, offered a strange kind of comfort. It was modern and sleek, with an air of excellence to everything—the diplomas and accolades lining the walls, the precision of the equipment, the quiet confidence of the staff. This was where the best doctors in the world came to practice, and looking at those credentials on the wall, I felt something in me settle for the first time since the call. If anyone could help me, it would be someone here.

When the neurosurgeon came in, he pulled up images of my brain on a large screen and began reviewing them one by one, explaining what he saw as he pointed to different areas on the scan. I sat there staring at the picture of my own skull, at the massive tumor the size of a racquetball sitting right in the center of my brain, and I couldn't quite believe what I was looking at. This thing had possibly been growing inside me for years, silently expanding while I went about my life completely unaware.

"At this point," the doctor said, studying the images, "I'm surprised you're functioning at all. I'm surprised you can even see."

I didn't know what to say to that. Carin sat beside me through all of it, meticulously taking notes so I wouldn't have to hold onto the details myself, handling the logistics so I could just do my best to absorb what was happening.

The doctor laid out the situation carefully. The tumor was pressing against my optic nerves and wrapped around a major artery, which meant surgery would be complicated—possibly requiring multiple procedures to remove it safely. I tried to take it all in, tried to prepare myself for whatever recovery lay ahead. Then he mentioned one final test. Most tumors like mine required surgical removal, he explained, but once in a blue moon, there were certain types that could be treated with medication alone. He didn't think I had that kind, based on my symptoms, but he wanted to rule it out before we scheduled anything.

"It's a long shot," he said. "But we won't know until we test for it."

That night, Carin and I sat together on the couch long after we should have gone to bed. We put on some soft music to calm our nerves. She held my hand, and every now and then she would squeeze it gently, just to remind me she was there.

We didn't talk much. What was there to say? The doctor had laid out the road ahead—multiple surgeries, weeks of recovery, the possibility of complications he had described in that calm, clinical way doctors use when they don't want to scare you but also can't lie. I had nodded along in his office as I understood, but now, in the quiet of our living room, the reality of it was starting to settle in.

"You okay?" Carin asked softly.

"I don't know," I said. "I keep trying to imagine what it's going to feel like. Someone cutting into my head. Being under anesthesia for hours. Waking up and not knowing if everything still works."

She didn't try to reassure me with words. She just leaned her head against my shoulder and stayed there.

At some point, we made our way to bed, but I don't think either of us really slept. I lay there in the dark, listening to Carin breathe beside me, and I thought about all the things I hadn't done yet. All the trips I hadn't taken. All the conversations I'd been putting off. I thought about my parents, both of them already struggling with their own health, and what it would do to them if something happened to me on that operating table.

And I prayed. Not for a miracle, exactly. Just for peace. Just for the strength to face whatever was coming.

God, I trust you.

Whatever happens, I trust you.

Somewhere in the early hours of the morning, I finally drifted off to sleep.

44

WINNING THE LOTTERY

THE NEXT MORNING, I WAS SITTING AT THE KITCHEN TABLE, A CUP OF coffee going cold in front of me, when my phone buzzed. I looked down and saw the neurosurgeon's number on the screen, and my heart seized up.

Carin saw my face and reached across the table to take my hand.

I answered the phone and braced myself.

"Des?" The doctor's voice sounded different than it had in his office—lighter somehow, almost excited. "Son, you're not going to believe this."

I gripped the phone tighter. "What is it?"

"You just won the lottery."

For a second, I didn't understand what he was saying. My mind was still prepared for the worst, still bracing for impact, and the words didn't compute.

"The test came back," he continued. "Not only do you not have cancer, you have the type of tumor that can be treated with medication. No surgery. You understand what I'm telling you? You don't need surgery."

I couldn't speak. I felt Carin squeeze my hand, her eyes locked on my face, trying to read what was happening.

"You're sure?" My voice came out hoarse. "You're absolutely sure?"

"I'm positive. Cancel everything. Find yourself a good endocrinologist, get on the right medications, and you're going to be fine. This is the best possible outcome, Des. I've been doing this a long time, and I don't get to make calls like this very often."

I thanked him over and over—and when I finally hung up the phone, I just sat there for a moment, staring at the screen, not quite believing what had just happened.

Then I looked up at Carin.

"I don't need surgery," I said. "I'm going to be okay."

Her face crumpled. She brought both hands to her mouth, and then she was crying—not sad tears, but the kind that come when you've been holding your breath for so long that you forgot what it felt like to exhale.

I pushed back from the table and threw my arms in the air, and Carin laid her head down on her arms and just wept—the kind of tears that come when you've been holding everything together and finally don't have to anymore. When she looked up at me, I pulled her into my arms and held her tight.

"I was so scared," she whispered into my shoulder. "I was so scared, Des. I didn't want to tell you how scared I was."

"I know," I said. "I know. But it's okay now. We're okay."

I spent the rest of that day on the phone. I called my parents first—my father kept saying "Thank God, thank God" over and over like a prayer. I called my brother and sister. I called my crew, one by one, and heard the relief in their voices.

That evening, Carin and I sat on the back deck, watching the sun go down over the water. The weight that had been pressing down on us for days had finally lifted, and all we wanted to do was sit in the lightness of it.

"You know what I keep thinking about?" I said after a while.

"What?"

"How close I came to not being here. Not just the tumor—everything. The hippo. The plane. FDNY. All of it."

I shook my head slowly. "I don't know why I've been spared so many times. But I'm done taking it for granted."

She reached over and took my hand. "You never did take it for granted. That's one of the things I love about you."

Within weeks, I began the medication, and it worked faster than anyone expected. My vision started coming back, slowly at first and then more clearly each day, until the world sharpened again into the place I remembered. I had resigned myself to the possibility that I might never captain my boats again, that the life I had built might be over, and now here I was, returning to it like a man given a second chance he hadn't dared to hope for.

My first day back was in late summer. I stepped aboard, and several customers were already there waiting. When they saw me, a few broke into smiles and reached out to shake my hand or pull me into a hug.

One of them was Joe, a Vietnam veteran who had become almost part of our crew over the years. Joe had an incredible strength and humility, the kind that comes from having seen too much and survived anyway. He was a decorated soldier who had escaped death more times than he could count, and he knew loss better than most people ever will. When he reached out his hand and then gave me a hug, I felt the weight of everything he carried, and everything I had just come through, pass between us without a word.

"We missed you, Des," he said. "More than you'll ever know. I'm so glad you're okay."

I thanked him, though my voice caught a little, and I made my way to the helm. The wheel felt solid under my hands, familiar and right, and as I looked out at the water stretching toward the horizon, I thought about something my father used to say. He had learned it the hard way, through his own long journey of injuries and recoveries as a firefighter, and he would repeat it to me sometimes when I was young, though I don't think I really understood it until now.

A healthy man has a thousand dreams, he would say. *A sick man has only one.*

Standing at the helm that morning, the sun on my face and the engine humming beneath my feet, I understood at last what he meant. All my dreams had narrowed to a single point during those terrible days—just let me live, just let me be okay—and now that I had been given that, everything else felt like grace. The boat, the water, the customers laughing on deck, the simple, ordinary miracle of another day: I had never been more grateful for any of it.

I was alive. I was well. And I got to go fishing—one more day.

45

THE GIFT OF NOW

I HEARD THEM BEFORE I SAW THEM. TWO VOICES, ONE STEADY AND ONE wavering, drifted through the screen door. "Amazing Grace," the second verse. I stopped on the porch steps and just listened.

Through the window, I could see them on the couch, heads bent over the old hymnal that had lived on my mother's bookshelf for as long as I could remember. Carin's arm was wrapped around Mom's shoulder, and Mom's finger traced the words as they sang, helping her keep her place. When they reached *"was blind but now I see,"* Mom's voice caught for just a moment before finding its way back.

I stood there, soaking in the moment.

In the weeks following the brain tumor diagnosis, life had taken on a different weight. The doctors had cleared me, the tumor was benign, and my vision had returned to normal. But something else had shifted, something harder to name. When you spend months wondering if you'll ever see clearly again, wondering if you'll be around to grow old, the ordinary moments stop feeling ordinary. And now that I was well, I found myself awake to everything I had nearly lost.

I made a promise to myself in those quiet weeks. I would stop rushing. I would stop letting small frustrations steal my peace. I would show up—really show up—for the people I loved, especially for my parents, whose time on this earth I knew was drawing shorter with each passing season.

Dad was in his rocking chair by the fireplace when I finally stepped inside, right where he'd been sitting for nearly fifty years. The little wood table beside him held the remains of his afternoon snack, a few crumbs from the butter cookies Carin had brought him earlier that morning. She'd discovered quickly that the bakery across the street from my boat carried all his old favorites, the same crumb cakes and cookies he used to pick up himself when he'd come down to the dock to visit me. Now that his legs wouldn't carry him that far anymore, she made the trip for him.

"She's a good woman," Dad said, nodding toward the living room where the singing continued. His voice was quieter than it used to be, but his eyes were sharp as ever.

"I know, Pop."

"What is she doing with a guy like you anyway?"

My dad always loved to bust my shoes.

"I don't know," I said. "And how the heck did Mom put up with you all these years?"

We both chuckled.

He reached out and squeezed my arm with those big hands of his. The strength in them had faded, but the warmth hadn't. His body was giving out—years of back injuries, a heart that required more and more procedures to keep beating steady—but his spirit remained. He could still holler at the television when the Yankees made a bad play, still shake his head at the evening news, and mutter about the state of politics. I was grateful for that. It meant he was still with us, still himself.

Mom was a different story.

The Alzheimer's had arrived quietly, the way fog rolls in off the water before you realize you can no longer see the shore. It started with small things. Misplaced keys. Repeated questions. Conversations that circled back on themselves within minutes. At first, we made excuses—she was tired, she had a lot on her mind—but over the past two years, the fog had thickened. Now there were moments when she struggled to follow a simple conversation, moments when the names of people she'd known for decades slipped just beyond her reach. We brought her to the doctors, tried every recommended treatment, and adjusted her medications. But it felt like trying to hold sand in your hands. No matter how tightly you gripped, it kept sliding through your fingers.

What the disease couldn't touch was her joy. Somewhere beneath the confusion, the woman she had always been still lived. Her face would light up at the sight of a cardinal on the feeder. She still laughed at my father's old jokes, even when she'd heard them a hundred times before. And when Carin sat beside her with the hymnal, Mom would close her eyes and sing from memory, the words returning to her from some deep place the Alzheimer's hadn't found.

Sometimes, if you let her talk, she would drift back even further, to the years before any of us existed. She'd grown up in a world I could barely imagine, the daughter of missionaries who'd raised her in Burma and India during the years surrounding the Second World War. Her childhood stories sounded like adventure novels—her family fleeing ahead of the Japanese advance, dodging submarines on the long voyage toward safety, trekking across India for weeks. Those experiences had shaped something essential in her, a lightness and wonder that never left her even as everything else began to fade.

Carin was captivated by those stories. She would sit with Mom for hours, asking gentle questions, letting her wander through her memories at whatever pace felt right. She never rushed her, never corrected her when the details got tangled. She just listened, and in the listening, she gave my mother a gift—the chance to be seen as the remarkable woman she had been, not just the fragile one she was becoming.

When the song ended, I heard them both laugh at something, and then Carin's voice said, "One more? How about 'How Great Thou Art'?"

I walked over to Dad's chair and sat on the arm of the couch across from him. Through the doorway, I could see Mom turning pages while Carin hummed the opening notes.

"Your poor mother," Dad said quietly, sadness in his eyes.

Then I followed his gaze to the living room, to my mother searching for the right page with trembling hands.

I nodded. I could see it too, the shape of what lay ahead. More doctors, more difficult conversations, more pieces of her slipping away. And Dad's own health was no sure thing. The rocking chair that had held him for fifty years might not hold him forever.

But that afternoon, with hymns floating through the house and the late light falling across my father's weathered hands, I made my peace with not knowing what came next. The storm would arrive when it arrived. For now, there was only this: the people I loved most in the world, all under one roof, all still here.

I closed my eyes and let the music wash over me, knowing these were the days I would someday ache to return to.

46

THE ANGELS COME AGAIN

Knowing how precious these days with my parents are, I made a point of dropping in to check on them as much as possible. Their house was on the way to the boat, so I made it part of my daily rhythm.

One morning, I walked through the door and was greeted by a beautiful smile on my mother's face.

"Son, look at all the birds! Aren't they amazing!" Mom's smile lit up the room as she pointed to the feeder.

"Beautiful, Mom." I put my arm around her as we watched together.

Though Alzheimer's had begun stealing her sharp mind, it hadn't touched her love of nature.

These morning coffee moments on the porch had become everything to me.

"This is the best part of my day," she said softly.

"Mine too, Momma."

We stood in comfortable silence, breathing in the birdsong echoing around us. I treasured every second, knowing that someday she might not remember who I was.

"Look! The first cardinal of the year! And a woodpecker!" She pointed excitedly.

"Magical," I whispered, squeezing her shoulder.

Too soon, I checked my watch. "I hate to go, but I've got eager fishermen waiting for me at the dock."

"Already? Well, go easy on those fish today."

"Promise." I kissed her cheek. "See you in a few hours."

"I'll be right here with my birds."

As I gathered my belongings, Mom shuffled onto the porch—fifteen feet above the ground, lined with the old white railings Dad had built years ago.

"Hello, beautiful birds!" she called out cheerfully.

I'm searching for my truck keys, realizing I must have mindlessly put them down when I came in."Mom, where did I put my keys?""No idea, Des. Sorry!"

I checked the truck. Nothing. Back inside, I rummaged across the countertops, growing anxious about the time.

"Mom, you sure—" I glanced up.

She's bending over the feeder. Hearing me, she stands abruptly—and suddenly loses her balance, arms pinwheeling.

"Mom!"

I sprint toward her, but she's already staggering backward toward the railing. Her legs give out completely. She falls, her head and torso smashing into the old wood. The railing explodes, lumber tearing away and tumbling to the ground below.

Somehow—impossibly—her body jolts forward from the impact, and her tailbone catches the very edge of the porch. She teeters there, suspended for one terrible heartbeat.

I'm only feet away, but it feels like miles. Time slows as I watch her begin to roll over the edge.

"Mom!"

I dive forward, grabbing her clothes with both hands. I pull with everything I have, dragging her back from the brink until she's safely away from the edge.

"Please tell me you're okay!" My hands shake as I check her over, adrenaline flooding through me.

She blinks up at me. "I think... I'm okay. Just dazed."

"You almost went over, Mom!" I pull her close, my whole body trembling.

"My legs just gave out when I stood up too fast." She pats my arm. "Thank God you were here."

"Thank God I couldn't find my keys. If I'd already left..." My voice trails off. I can't finish the thought.

She smiles weakly. "Someone was looking out for me today. Those angels hid your keys."

I just nodded, stunned.

I supported her weight as she rose slowly. "Take my arm."

I walked her carefully to her chair and brought her water. Once she was settled, I retreated to my office, needing a moment to breathe. My hands wouldn't stop shaking.

Thirty seconds. That's all that separated me from losing her forever.

I returned to the porch and knelt beside her chair. From now on, I would hold her a little tighter, hug her a little longer, and never take a single bird-watching morning for granted.

Thank God for lost keys.Thank God I was here.

Thank God the Angels came again.

47

SITTING VIGIL

THE KIDS' LAUGHTER RANG OUT ACROSS THE DOCK AS THEY SCRAMBLED OFF the boat, their voices carrying that particular joy that comes from a day on the water with no responsibilities beyond holding a fishing rod. I watched them file up the gangway toward their waiting school bus, backpacks bouncing, already telling each other exaggerated stories about the ones that got away. It had been a good trip. Just another ordinary afternoon.

Then my phone rang. I recognized my parents' health aide's voice immediately, and something in her tone made me brace before she even got the words out. "Your father's in bad shape—he can barely walk, he's confused, and he's having trouble breathing. I've called an ambulance. They're taking him to the hospital."

I grabbed my gear and bolted off the boat without looking back. By the time I reached the cardiac hospital, Dad was already fading in and out. His heart had been giving him trouble for years, but this was something more. His liver was failing now, too.

They hooked him up to everything—monitors, IVs, wires running from his chest to screens that translated his life into jagged green lines. I sat at his bedside and held his hand.

My brother John flew in from Oregon the moment he heard, dropping everything, as did my sister, who headed down from upstate New York. Carin came and sat with me for hours whenever she could, her presence a quiet comfort in that sterile room. We surrounded Dad with as much love and prayer as we could offer while the doctors worked to bring him back.

Dad couldn't speak. All he could do was writhe with discomfort, stopping only to mumble sounds none of us could understand. I held his hand through all of it, praying the only prayer I could manage: God, let Your will be done. Be with my father no matter what. If he's meant to live, give him strength. And whatever happens, let his soul be at peace.

Then, as if things weren't bad enough, my brother called. He'd gone home to check on Mom and found her in bad shape—she'd fallen hard and broken several vertebrae. They were taking her to the hospital. "I'll handle this side," he said. "You stay with Dad."

I put my head against the wall and forced myself to exhale. All I could do was focus on my father while my brother handled Mom.

For three days, Dad drifted somewhere between this world and beyond. I barely left his side, terrified that if I stepped away, I would miss the moment—either the moment he came back to us, or the moment he slipped away for good.

After nearly three days, finally a ray of hope. I had been dozing at his bedside when I heard him stir and snapped fully awake. Dad's eyes opened, just enough to find me.

"Son," he said, his voice rough but unmistakably his own. "What the hell am I doing here?"

Tears rolled down my face before I could stop them. "Dad? You're back?"

"Yeah, son. What the hell is going on?"

A doctor stepped in. "So great to see you speaking again, Mr. O'Sullivan. You had a rough few days."

"When the hell can I get out of here?" Dad asked.

"Soon enough," the doctor said, smiling. "His liver is stabilizing. His heart function is improving. I think he's through the worst of it."

Over the following days, Dad slowly regained his strength. Meanwhile, my brother, sister, and I took shifts between two hospitals. Mom had broken several vertebrae, but her prognosis was good.

Nearly dying rearranges priorities. Dad wasn't a man who said I love you easily. He showed it through action. But now, he kept reaching for my hand, telling me how proud he was of his kids.

One afternoon, sunlight pouring through the window, he squeezed my hand. "Son, I am the luckiest Dad in the world."

"Come on, Dad."

"I mean it. Watching you kids live good lives—that's everything." Then he said, quietly, "You know one of the happiest moments of my life? That day we caught all those striped bass together."

I wasn't expecting that.

"Watching you run down that beach, smiling ear to ear… that made every sacrifice worth it."

And then my father—the stoic man that he was—began to tear up. I squeezed his hand tighter.

"Thank you, son," he said. "I'm proud of you. And I love you with all my heart."

"I love you too, Dad."

We didn't say too much after that, as Dad's eyes slowly closed and he drifted back to sleep. That moment with him, though, is one I will carry with me for the rest of my life.

48

THE NEW NORMAL

AGAINST ALL ODDS, THEY RELEASED BOTH MY PARENTS FROM THE HOSPITAL on the same day. That alone felt like a small miracle. We got them settled that first night home—Mom on the sofa with a blanket over her legs, Dad easing into his rocking chair, the same chair he'd sat in for fifty years. Even though he was still weak, even though he needed help getting up and down the stairs, he was home. And that meant everything.

John, Kait, and I drifted into the kitchen to start on dinner. We moved around each other without saying much, all feeling relieved to finally be home. At some point, we all stopped and looked at each other, and there it was—that dazed, exhausted, grateful look passing between us. No words. Just the shared weight of the week we had survived.

The Clancy Brothers played from the speakers. I stood at the stove putting the finishing touches on dinner—steak with all the fixings, mashed potatoes with extra butter. The smell of seared meat, garlic, and rosemary filled the kitchen, and I caught myself smiling as I turned the steaks. We made it, I thought. Jesus... we actually made it.

Dad was watching all of it from his chair with a look of quiet contentment on his face—the look of a man surrounded by his children, in his own home, after a battle he wasn't sure he would survive.

I was just about to call everyone to the table when Kait's voice cut through the music.

"Momma? You hear me?"

I turned from the stove. Kait was leaning toward our mother, her voice rising. "Momma, what's wrong?"

Mom had begun to lean to one side, her body tilting slowly, unnaturally, falling over the side of the sofa. I crossed the room and saw it—the corner of her mouth pulling downward, the left side of her face starting to sag. The aide moved quickly, shut off the music, and in the sudden silence, we all understood.

Dad sat helpless in his rocking chair, still too weak to stand on his own, watching his wife of fifty years have a stroke ten feet away from him. He called over to her, his voice cracking. "Just hang in there, Mom. We love you."

I called 911. My hands were shaking. The minutes stretched out impossibly long as we gathered around her, doing what little we could. The steak sat forgotten on the counter, going cold.

I knelt beside Dad and put my hand on his arm. "We've got her, Dad. She's going to be okay."

I wasn't sure I believed it—but he needed to hear it.

For the second time in a week, we loaded her into an ambulance and followed its lights through the night. She lay in the emergency room for hours, drifting in and out, mumbling sounds we couldn't understand. Her broken back still caused her pain, and now this new thief had come for her mind.

I had just finished filling out paperwork when Carin suggested we sing to her. I knew immediately it was right.

Mom had always loved to sing. It was her favorite part of church every Sunday—standing proud, letting her soprano voice ring out with all the spirit she had in her. What came through was something truer than technique—her joy, her faith, her beautiful, stubborn aliveness. For years, she and I had shared that love. On quiet evenings, I would sit at the old upright piano she had bought me as a boy, and we would open the hymn book together, her voice soaring while my fingers found the chords.

Now, in this hospital room, Carin and I began to sing. "How Great Thou Art." Then "Amazing Grace."

Mom couldn't speak. She barely knew where she was. But when the music started, her lips began to move. She mumbled the words, finding them somewhere in the deep places the stroke had not touched. A gentle smile came to her face. Somewhere beneath the damage, the memories of a lifetime still lived—her childhood as a missionary's daughter in Burma and India, all those Sunday mornings with the choir, all those evenings around the piano with her son.

The spirit remembers what the mind forgets.

Around midnight, Carin slipped out and came back with two cups of hot tea. John and Kait had gone home to rest, and the two of us kept vigil. We didn't talk much. But every now and then I would look across the bed at Carin, and she would meet my eyes with that quiet, steady look. After the week I'd had, that unspoken presence meant more than I could say.

It was three in the morning by the time they got her to a room. Her eyes were closed, but her face looked peaceful. And still, under her breath, she was singing—the soft refrain of a song she loved called "So Much Magnificence."

I tucked her blanket around her and kissed her forehead. Then I stepped back toward the door, kissed my hand, and sent one last kiss floating through the air toward her bed.

"I love you, Mama," I said.

I turned and walked out into the hallway, not knowing what tomorrow would bring.

***

THE WEEKS that followed were a blur of rehab facilities and careful conversations with doctors. Slowly, Mom regained enough of herself that they agreed she could come home. Dad needed care, too—his body was failing, but his mind remained sharp, which was perhaps its own kind of burden.

We moved Mom into a bedroom downstairs and resigned ourselves to the work ahead—aides, doctor's appointments, medication schedules, daily battles large and small. We tried to find grace in it all.

Sometimes, when life gets hard, angels appear. For our family, that angel was my Mom's lifelong friend, Paula. When Paula appeared, Mom would snap back to us, turn with a smile that seemed to come from somewhere deeper than her confusion could reach, and call out, "Paula!" It happened every time. No matter how lost my mother seemed, Paula's arrival brought her back.

The two of them had been like sisters for as long as I could remember. For years, they worked side by side in my mother's catering business—cooking together, laughing together. Now Paula limped in on her bad hip, the one that had been through multiple surgeries, and she never said a word about it. She had known her own share of hardship, but complaint was not in her nature. She just showed up, day after day.

My sister Kait made the downstairs room feel like home—photographs on the walls, her favorite blankets piled on the bed, familiar trinkets on the nightstand.

Dad still insisted on sleeping upstairs in his own bedroom. We installed a track chair on the staircase, but he fought us on it constantly. He did not want to admit what was happening to his body, and I could not blame him.

One afternoon, I served him lunch at the kitchen table—his favorite ham sandwich, an iced coffee, and a couple of Oreo cookies for dessert. I told him to sit and relax while I made some business calls. But a few minutes in, I caught movement in the corner of my vision. Dad had gotten up and was shuffling toward the stairs with his walker.

I ended my call and rushed over to find him already a few steps up, both hands gripping the railings, his knees trembling. The wooden stairs were old and slippery, and one wrong step could have sent him tumbling.

"Dad, what are you doing? Just sit in the track chair."

He turned and looked at me, and there was a fierceness in his eyes that I recognized from the strong man he used to be.

"I'm not giving up that easy, son. I have to keep trying. Once I can't walk up these stairs, I don't even want to think what my life will be like."

My heart broke for him. I tried to imagine what it must feel like to arrive at that stage of life, after decades of strength, and to find that your great mountain to climb was now a single flight of stairs in your own home.

The argument drained out of me. I moved behind him and placed one hand gently on his back, and I stayed there as he climbed. What should have taken thirty seconds took several minutes. He gripped the railings and pulled himself up one step at a time, his whole body working for each small victory, and I matched his pace without a word.

When he reached the top, we walked together into his bedroom, and he lowered himself onto the edge of his bed. I knelt and untied his shoes, slipped them off, and swung his legs up onto the mattress. I pulled the blanket over him and tucked it around his shoulders.

As I turned to leave, he reached out and grasped my hand. His arm, once so powerful, felt thin now, but his grip was still firm.

"Son," he said quietly as I covered his hand with mine. "I know it's really hard for you right now."

I felt tears welling up. I nodded, leaned down, and kissed him on the forehead as he squeezed my hand tighter. We both took a breath. I laid his hand back over his heart and gently let go. I stood there a moment longer, watching his eyes close, and then I slipped out of the room, my heart aching.

This was now the new normal.

NOT EVERY DAY carried that kind of weight, but none of them were easy. Mom fell more often now, and each time it shook something loose in me.

One afternoon, Paula called while I was out running errands for the boat. I rushed home to find my mother on the kitchen floor, propped against the cabinets where she'd been sitting for nearly twenty minutes. She looked dazed, but when she saw me, she forced a smile.

"Desi. I am so glad you are here."

I tried to make light of it, the way we'd learned to do. "Mom, what are you doing on the floor again? We have all these comfortable chairs."

She laughed. I got my hands under her arms, scooped her up, and eased her back into her wheelchair, then wheeled her to her room and got her settled. But after the door clicked shut behind me, I felt the weight pressing down. Watching your parents become helpless wounds you in a place you didn't know existed.

I drove home to my condo to clear my head before going back to the boats.

A friend had given me a framed quote from Mother Teresa that Carin and I kept on our kitchen counter:

"I used to pray that God would feed the hungry, or do this or that. But now I pray that He will guide me to do whatever I'm supposed to do—what I can do. I used to pray for answers, but now I'm praying for strength."

In the hardest moments, I would say silently: Please, God. Just give me strength.

But that afternoon, the practice wasn't enough. These grueling months were just getting to me. Anger, sadness, hopelessness—and worst of all, a resentment I fought hard not to feel. Some days, you win the battle to stay positive. Some days, your humanity gets the best of you.

I parked at my condo and got out to walk, hoping the air might clear my head.

And that was when I saw Tom.

49

THANK YOU

I HAD JUST PARKED AT MY CONDO WHEN I SAW TOM WHEELING HIMSELF UP the mild slope that runs past my building, pushing hard against the grade, a hundred feet away. My mind was still churning from my mother on the kitchen floor, from the weight of these grinding months, and part of me just wanted to walk alone and shake something loose. But Tom's wave caught me—that big, infectious sweep of his arm—and his voice rang out across the distance.

"Hello, neighbor!" he called. "What a magnificent day, isn't it?"

I walked toward him, and by the time I reached his wheelchair, he was grinning ear to ear, his face lit up like a man with so much to be happy about.

"Today is just the best day to be alive," Tom said. "The sun is shining, the birds are out, and I already did a hundred crunches this morning if you can believe it."

Tom has lived as a quadriplegic since he was eighteen years old. He is in his fifties now, which means he has known the better part of his life from that wheelchair. His legs are thin from decades of sitting, but he wears shorts anyway, and a T-shirt, and he loves to position himself in the sun until his skin turns a deep bronze. It is one of the only pleasures left to him—just sitting there, feeling the warmth beat down on his face.

"A hundred crunches?" I said. "How the heck did you do that?"

"Watch!" His face lit up with pride as he slowly lifted his right knee, barely six inches off the wheelchair, while bringing his left shoulder partway down. The two never came close to meeting. But for Tom, it counted.

"Did you see that?" he said. "I did a hundred of those already today!"

I stood there, looking at this man who could barely move, who was smiling as if he had been handed the world, and something cracked open in me. All the dark thoughts I had been wrestling with—the anger, the sadness, the resentment I fought so hard not to feel—they just stopped. Here was a man celebrating six inches of movement, filled with gratitude for what his broken body could still do. So what exactly was I so upset about?

"Wow, Tom. That's so awesome, my friend. I'm so glad you're having a great day."

"I wish I could go on the boat with you," he said.

"One day for sure, Tom. One day for sure."

We shared a few more words, and then I put my hand on his shoulder. "Great seeing you today," I said.

He tried to raise his arm a few inches to wave. "Have a great day, Captain."

"Thanks, Tom. You take care, my friend."

I started my truck and pulled out onto the road, still turning over what had just happened. Tom had snapped me out of my fog the way a cold wave snaps you awake, and I realized I did not want to spend another moment lamenting the hardships that lay ahead.

I drove to the marina and parked, but instead of heading straight to work, I walked to the bench that overlooks the bulkhead—the bench where my father loved to sit and watch the boats rock in their slips. I sat down and took a breath.

The sun was warm on my face. I sat there watching my crew—these loyal men and women who showed up day after day, who cared for these boats and for each other, who had become family—and I felt gratitude begin to pour into the hollow places Tom had cracked open.

I thought of Captain Chris, who had worked tirelessly for me for over 20 years, never once missing a day of work or being late. I thought of Captain Mark, now with me nearly 17 years, who gave up life in the corporate world to come work for me. He is as honest, kind, and devoted as anyone I have ever met, and he has treated this company as if it were his own.

I thought of Bernadette, in the office, who had been with me for nearly two decades, day in and day out, took great pride in her work, and helped me grow the business, all while she raised her two children through the ups and downs of motherhood.

I thought of Jared, our mechanic who had grown up on the boats with us and had worked for me for many years. Jared, more times than I can possibly count, answered the phone at some late hour to help us with whatever mechanical problems we had. Without him, I don't know what we would have done.

I thought of all the great deckhands and captains who helped me over the years, like Paulie, Mike, Matt, Dom, Jon, Alex, Brian, Don, and so many more, not to mention my wonderful office team, Susan and Amy, who answered thousands of phone calls for us. Such incredible young men and women, each leaving their little mark on this beautiful company.

Tom had given me something I didn't know I needed — a reset. Not a fix, not an answer, just a shift in the lens. And through that lens, sitting on my father's bench, I could suddenly see what had been there all along: the life I had built, the people who had chosen to build it with me, all the blessings I had been too buried to notice.

None of that had changed. Only my eyes had changed.

I took a long breath, stood up, and walked down to the boat — a smile, finally, returning to my face.

And with that, I felt ready to fight another day.

50

DOUBLE ANCHORED

My epiphany with Tom shifted something within my heart, and the weeks that followed began to carry a different weight. Quieter. Softer. Easier.

Carin and I also settled into a rhythm we hadn't known we were missing—planting a garden together, cooking meals that stretched into long evenings, taking walks that had no destination and no hurry. We laughed more than we had in months, the kind of silly, unguarded laughter that comes when you finally stop bracing for the next blow. My parents were still fading, slowly, the way autumn fades into winter. But somewhere in the midst of all that tending—the garden, the meals, each other—I started to feel something I hadn't felt in a long time.

Peace.

We were sitting over dinner one night when Carin looked at me and said what we'd both been thinking.

"Let's not wait," I said.

She knew exactly what I meant. After everything we'd been through—the sabotage, the brain tumor, my parents in the ICU, the long nights of caregiving—we'd learned something that takes some people a lifetime to understand. The days are numbered. They always were, but now we could feel it. And what were we waiting for?

We were in love. We had gotten engaged a few weeks before. We knew we were right for each other, without question. My parents were still here, still able to share in the joy of their son's wedding—but for how much longer? We had figured we'd get married sometime down the line, months from now. But this moment of inspiration hit us both.

"This summer," I said. "Before anything else happens."

She reached across the table and took my hand.

"Absolutely," she said. "This summer."

* * *

I WOKE on the morning of my wedding with butterflies in my stomach, though it was more eager anticipation than nerves. I stepped out onto the porch of my condo and looked up into a clear blue sky, so grateful we'd been blessed with beautiful weather. A gentle August breeze moved through the trees. It was going to be a perfect day.

We kept things simple. The ceremony would be in my parents' backyard at the home where I grew up, the same house I'd galloped out of as a boy with my fishing rod in hand, running down to the beach below. My dear friend John had built us a white pergola as his wedding gift, and we'd adorned it with flowers and set it at the end of my father's rose garden, right at the edge of the small cliff overlooking the harbor. From where I would stand to say my vows, I could see the very stretch of shoreline where I'd caught that striped bass with my dad so many years before.

I wore shorts and bare feet out there in the garden, surrounded by my father's flowers. My brother stood beside me. Captain Paul and Michelle—the same Michelle who had introduced me to Carin at the health center—officiated together, both interfaith ministers, both dear friends. A string quartet began to play Pachelbel's Canon.

I looked up toward the porch.

There she was.

Carin appeared at the top of the stairs in her white dress, a wreath of flowers in her blonde hair, her father proudly holding her arm. She looked like an angel. As she descended the very steps I used to run down as a boy, her bright smile never wavered. And when her eyes found mine across the lawn, I felt my breath catch.

Seeing the woman you love walk toward you on your wedding day is a moment you will never forget. The world goes quiet. Time stretches. And somewhere in your chest, you feel the click of something falling into place that you didn't even know was missing.

Her father placed her hand in mine. I could feel the tears on my cheeks. My Mom and Dad, with the help of my brother and sister, had made it down to the garden and sat right in front of us. It was a good day for both of them—one of those gifts you learn to cherish when your parents' health is fragile. My mother's eyes were clear and happy, and every time I caught her gaze during the ceremony, it warmed my heart. They were here. They were present. They, too, had dreamed of this day for years.

Paul and Michelle had gathered sand from the beach below us—the beach where I'd grown up fishing—and sand from the south shore of Long Island, where Carin had grown up, the same shore where she'd taken that long walk praying for God to bring her a good man. During the ceremony, they combined the two sands in a beautiful Waterford chalice, the grains mingling together the way our lives were mingling now.

When it came time for vows, I spoke from my heart. I talked about how I'd dreamed my whole life of meeting the love of my life, how I never could have imagined someone as radiant, loving, and compassionate as her stepping forward to be my bride. I spoke about the many roads we'd both traveled before we were ready to find each other, the healing that had to happen before our hearts could recognize what they'd been searching for. I promised to love her and care for her with all my soul, to laugh with her always, to stand beside her no matter what.

And then Carin offered hers.

She began with Rumi.

"The minute I heard my first love story, I started looking for you, not knowing how blind that was. Lovers don't finally meet somewhere. They're in each other all along."

Her voice was steady but full of emotion as she told the story I'd first heard on our date at Tula's Kitchen, the story that had stopped my heart then and stopped it again now.

"When I was a young girl in Montauk," she said, "I remember looking for my husband. Years later, on the first sunny day of spring, I would drive out east and walk the docks because I felt you were somewhere near **The Dock**."

The Dock. That weathered dive bar where fishermen still in their boots and hooded sweatshirts gathered to swap reports and catch up on local scuttlebutt. The same bar where my buddies and I had eaten lunch nearly every day during my years in Montauk.

"I looked for you for a very long time," she continued, "until one day I realized I had to find you within my own heart. I had to grow into my true, whole self to meet you as your loving partner."

She spoke about the day she walked the beach and prayed for a good man—and how God and the angels had answered her prayer. She spoke about how there was no doubt in her mind that a more perfect partner could have been designed for her.

And then she said something that made my throat tighten.

"I think about you as a young boy playing piano with your family. I think of you as if it were my own dream—the vision of you running off the school bus, down the side of the house with your fishing pole, to this very beach."

She gestured toward the water below us.

"I smile as if I am looking back on the other half of my love story."

I stood there with tears streaming down my face, understanding for the first time what it meant that she had been searching for me all those years—just as I had been searching for her.

Following my heart hadn't just brought me the life of my dreams. It had led me to someone who had been following her heart too—both of us divinely guided toward the same place.

Later, my brother John stood to give his toast.

"I think of all the things we've done together," he began. "Growing up, fishing this harbor, playing sports, traveling. You're an amazing brother, and it's an honor to stand here today."

He paused and smiled.

"One thing Des's fishermen friends always said was, 'We don't know who he'll marry, but we're pretty sure she'll be able to double anchor a boat.'"

Laughter rippled through the guests.

"They teased him for years that he just needed that perfect person, even one who could double anchor a boat. Now here's the thing about double anchoring. When it's rough out, when the currents are wrong, when the wind kicks up, captains sometimes need to put out two anchors. And what those two anchors do is let you adjust, reposition, and stay steady when the seas are at their worst."

He turned to Carin.

"Now, I'm pretty sure you can't actually double anchor a boat. But what I've seen from you—through your love and compassion for my family—is that you brought stability. You brought comfort. You brought incredible love during some very hard times."

His voice cracked.

"Marriage is the give and the go, the push and the pull. Sometimes one anchor holds. Sometimes the other does. But you always need both —because when the winds shift, the other anchor will need to take the load. Just like you did for my brother."

He raised his glass.

"To the bride and groom. May your seas be mostly calm—but when they're not, may you remember you're stronger together."

As the afternoon stretched toward evening, I danced with my mother.

The sun poured down warm and golden, and she looked up at me with a clarity I hadn't seen in months. It was as if her Alzheimer's had simply stepped aside for these few hours, granting her full presence on the day her son married. She knew exactly where we were. She knew exactly why.

She put her hand on my cheek.

"Des," she said softly. "I am just so happy right now."

I held her close and swayed, thanking God for this moment—for giving her the joy of seeing her boy find the love of his life, clear-eyed and full of happiness.

Near the end of the day, my father made his way to the microphone.

Family legend held that he had won my mother's heart over fifty years earlier by singing *"I'll Take You Home Again, Kathleen."* And as he liked to joke, for some reason, she believed him.

Throughout my life—on mom's birthday, on Mother's Day—he would ask me to sit at the piano and accompany him as he sang that song to her in his beautiful tenor voice.

Now his hands were shaky. His voice was a far cry from what it once was. But he took the microphone anyway and sang with all his heart.

I'll take you home again, Kathleen…

The notes came out trembling but true, carrying fifty years of love and loyalty and shared roads. Every guest fell silent.

When the last note faded, my mother reached out both arms.

My father went to her and wrapped her in a hug.

There wasn't a dry eye in the house.

I stood there watching them hold each other—the firefighter and the missionary's daughter—and understood how one heart leads to another, how one act of courage becomes a family, how love carries forward.

Somehow, on this winding road of life, it all works out in the end.

Not the way you plan.

Not the way you expect.

But if you follow your heart, if you trust the currents you cannot see—

Somehow, you arrive exactly where you were always meant to be.

Double anchored.

Steady in the storm.

Home.

EPILOGUE

As I pulled out of the driveway of my childhood home for the last time in the fall of 2025, all I could think about was the last five years and what a whirlwind it had been.

Some parts were amazing. Five years of marriage, of building a life with Carin, our beautiful home we built, and our dogs. Waking up each morning a few miles from the boats and feeling that same quiet hum of gratitude that had carried me through everything. Celtic Quest kept growing. We opened two new locations out on the east end of Long Island—one in Peconic Bay, another in eastern Long Island Sound—and the company I had once worried might not survive its first season now stretched across the waters I had fished my whole life. Twenty-five seasons and counting. Hard to believe. Seemed like only yesterday that Neil and I were sinking in that dinghy on day one, soaking wet and wondering if we'd made a terrible mistake.

Many of the men and women who helped me build Celtic Quest were still by my side, some having invested nearly two decades of loyalty and devotion in a company they ran as if it were their own. They had families now. Kids who grew up on the boats the same way I grew up in the firehouse. These people had given me their best years, and in return, Celtic Quest had helped them build lives they were proud of. I never took that for granted. Not for a single day.

Through it all, Carin was my anchor. Through the long days and the hard seasons, through the weight of what was coming next, she was steady and constant and full of a quiet grace that I leaned on more than she probably knew. She would drive over to my parents' house with fresh treats from the bakery, or simply sit beside my mother and listen to music together, treating my parents as her own. When I came home exhausted from caregiving, running the business, and holding everything together, she held me. That is what true love and devotion look like. Not the grand gestures. The showing up. Sitting beside someone when they need you most.

We needed every bit of that devotion because the years that followed were the hardest of my life.

COVID came first, and with it a kind of isolation none of us had ever known. My father, already battling the wear of age—bad knees, a failing heart, the stubborn remnants of a body that had given everything it had to the fire department and to his family—ended up in the hospital for months with a severe knee infection. We weren't allowed to visit. The only way to see him was to intercept him on the way to a doctor's appointment, outpatient, grabbing whatever stolen minutes we could in a parking lot.

One day, I got word that Dad had an orthopedic appointment scheduled. I hatched a plan. I loaded up my mom, my sister Kait, and my dad's beloved chocolate lab, Rosie—his very best friend in those later years—and we drove to the medical building and waited in the parking lot like a family of stowaways. When they wheeled Dad out into the sunlight, the five of us had our reunion right there between the parked cars and the handicap ramps. He smiled when he saw us. But I think he smiled the most when Rosie bounded up and put her head in his lap. Some things don't need words.

Rosie brought such joy and comfort to all of us through these hard times. Sadly, though, she was the first to leave us. Cancer. She died peacefully in our home, the way she lived — surrounded by the people who loved her. Even though she couldn't walk, she still nudged her favorite tennis ball back and forth with her nose to us before the vet gently put her to sleep.

My Dad and I carried her out to the driveway after she passed. My father is not a man who cries. In my whole life, I had seen it happen once — in the days after 9/11, when even the strongest men I knew let something through.

Until Rosie.

Tears rolled down his face. He didn't try to stop them. She had been his best friend through the hardest years of his life. She had asked nothing and given him everything, the way only a truly loyal dog can do.

And then something happened that I still think about. Just as we stood there, a small group of sparrows appeared, four or five of them, and began flying in a figure eight, slow and deliberate, right above us. Again and again. A figure eight. The infinity sign. The great circle of life, right there above our driveway. I know animals go to heaven. But it felt like she wasn't just leaving — but becoming part of this world too, of the life force that moves through all things. A beautiful being had died, and it truly felt like God was welcoming her home.

Carin and I had recently adopted another dog, Sunny, not long before we lost Rosie. A golden retriever puppy who had already worked her way into the center of everything, the way puppies do.

One afternoon, when Sunny was about six months old, Carin was walking her through downtown Port Jefferson when a motorcycle rumbled past, and Sunny took off. Carin let her pull and just followed, curious where this little dog thought she needed to go. Of all the places in that whole village, Sunny ran straight down Main Street, made several turns, then headed directly to the marina, down the ramp, and right to the boarding ladder of the Celtic Quest— a place she had visited only once in her life two months before. She looked for me, but I was out on the Sound, fishing.

Carin stood there at the edge of my dock, catching her breath, and felt something familiar wash over her — that quiet certainty of being close to someone she couldn't quite reach. She had stood like this before, years ago, on a dock in Montauk, long before she ever knew my name, drawn there by something she couldn't explain but trusted all the same.

I think sometimes about the sparrows tracing their slow circle above Rosie, and the little golden dog who somehow found her way to my boat, and the force that pulled Carin to a dock in Montauk all those years before any of us had met — and I know there is a thread running through all of it, quiet and invisible, that knows where we are meant to be long before we do. Knowing that always brings me comfort.

MOM WAS the next to go.

She had fought Alzheimer's for years, that cruelest of thieves, the one that takes you from yourself piece by piece while your body keeps going. We set up a hospice bed in the back of the house and cared for her around the clock as she slowly, gently slipped away. It was a long vigil, and it was sacred.

In the months before she passed, word had gotten out that Mom wasn't well. And random people she knew began to call from her long and varied life.

One of them was named Yung. Years ago, he came over from China when he was around twenty, barely spoke a word of English, worked sixteen-hour days at a Chinese restaurant, had no family in this country, and no one to lean on. My mother had found him the way she found everyone who needed finding. She invited him to the house on his one day off each week, and the two of them would sit together while she helped him learn English. Afterward, she'd take him down to the beach where he loved to dig for clams and mussels, and he'd cook them up, and they'd sit and talk about life in his broken English and her infinite patience. She taught him to drive her own car. She helped him get his license. She even helped him buy his first van on Craigslist so he could start a small seafood distribution business.

That small business now runs a fleet of twenty trucks up and down the eastern seaboard, with a factory and a thriving operation. Yung is married with a beautiful family, living the American dream in every sense of the word.

When he heard my mother was fading, he packed up his wife and children and drove five hours from Pennsylvania to our house. He wanted his family to meet the woman who had changed his life.

He knelt beside her bed and took her hand. She placed her other hand over his. Even through the fog of the disease, she knew exactly who he was. She smiled, and in that smile was everything—all the time they had spent together, the driving lessons, the van on Craigslist, a young man's whole future unlocked by the simplest kind of love.

"Teacher," he said softly. "I just want to thank you for everything you did for me."

It was how he always addressed her. Every phone call, every message over the years—"Hello, Teacher." I sat on the sofa across the room, barely holding myself together, watching his wife and children standing behind him, witnessing this moment that said more about my mother's life than any eulogy ever could.

SHE PASSED IN 2024, and we held her memorial service in the place she had helped build—the village community center on the waterfront in Port Jefferson. She had worked tirelessly alongside the mayor and so many others to bring that building into existence, and her energy was infused in every beam and window of the place. It was the only fitting venue to say goodbye.

The July sun beamed through the giant bay windows and lit the conference room in gold as it overlooked Port Jefferson Harbor. Person after person rose to speak, and each story revealed another facet of this extraordinary woman. She had helped restore the oyster beds in our local harbors. She had organized beach cleanups for years. She helped build a wooden boat shop on the waterfront dedicated to preserving Port Jefferson's boat-building heritage. She helped found and run multiple festivals in the village, and every shop owner on Main Street knew my mom and her beautiful smile. The most common thing people said was simply, "I just felt happier after talking to Kathy O'Sullivan."

Perhaps her greatest legacy was the annual Charles Dickens Festival, which she helped launch, along with the mayor and several dedicated friends, nearly 30 years ago. To this day, every December, thousands of families pour into the village of Port Jefferson to celebrate the Christmas season among the carolers, the winter scenes, and the spirit of the holiday brought to life in the streets. That festival has been going strong for almost three decades now, and if you listen closely on a cold December night as the bells ring and the carols echo off the storefronts, you can still hear her spirit sprinkling fairy pixie dust in every note.

One man rose to speak who I didn't expect. He wasn't from the committees, the festivals, or the civic organizations. He was a man who had come to Port Jefferson as a young university student, going through a hard stretch of life, feeling sad, alone, and unsure of what to do next. My mother, being my mother, had befriended him. She used to take him out to lunch now and then, just to keep him company. Such a simple gesture. A meal and a conversation, nothing more.

He stood in that sunlit room and looked out at all of us and said, "I have traveled the world studying with spiritual teachers and gurus—all the people you would think would be the most influential in a person's life. And among all of them, I would say that your mom ranks right at the very top."

The room went still. And in that stillness, every person there understood what kind of woman we had lost.

AFTER MOM DIED, the house became eerily quiet.

Dad sat in his rocking chair by the fireplace, the same chair he had settled into for decades, and the silence pressed in around him. He didn't talk about it much. That wasn't his way. But once in a while, he would turn to you and say, in that plain, honest voice of his, "You know, I'm just glad mom's suffering is over now. I pray she's at peace."

The year that followed was a slow unraveling. Dad's heart was giving out. His back, which had never fully recovered from the injury that ended his fire career all those decades ago, had deteriorated to the point where he could barely stand. I was lifting him under his arms and lowering him into a wheelchair just to move him from one room to the next. And yet the man himself—his spirit, his fight, his stubbornness—that never wavered. Not once.

On many a day, he would still argue that he wanted to drive his car to get a haircut or buy lunch at his favorite deli. His fighting spirit kept him in denial of his failing body.

On one afternoon—an ordinary day, nothing to mark it as different from any other—that spirit shifted. I had brought him lunch and gotten him settled in his rocking chair, and I knelt down beside him the way I always did. He looked at me, and I looked at him, and for the first time in my entire life, something deep in me simply just knew. I could feel it. In that moment, I knew that my dad would be leaving us soon.

In all my years of caring for him, I had never felt anything like it. It hit me so profoundly that I could barely hold myself together. Twice that afternoon, I had to step outside and take a walk just to center myself, because the last thing Dad needed was to see me falling apart. That had always been my way—hold it together in front of them, melt down on your own time afterward. But this time was different. My heart knew something my mind was still trying to deny. I could barely hold back the tears.

Later that evening, I scooped him up under his arms, got him into the wheelchair, and wheeled him across the room to his hospice bed—the same room where his rocking chair sat, the same room with the fireplace he had loved for years, the room where we used to sit by the fire as a family while mom brought out one of her amazing dinners and the sound of Irish songs filled the house. I tucked him in and got him as comfortable as I could, adjusting the pillows, pulling the blankets up the way he liked them.

Then he looked at me and said something he had never once said in his entire life.

"Son, do you think you could give me a little oxygen? It's kind of hard to breathe right now."

And that was when I knew for certain. This man, who had carried people out of burning buildings, who had never once in ninety years asked for help if he could avoid it—he was telling me, in the only way he knew how, that the fight was almost over.

I set up his oxygen and made sure he was comfortable. Then he raised his arm the way he always did and put up his hand.

"Come on," he said. "Give me one last arm wrestle before you go."

Even then. Even at the very end. Those big, powerful hands of his, the same hands that had gripped fire hoses and swung axes, still had some strength left in them. I wrapped my hand around his and let him beat me one last time.

Then I leaned down, kissed him on the forehead, hugged him as tight as I could, and told him I loved him.

That was the last time I would see him alive.

My dad's breathing became more and more labored with each passing hour, and his health aide began frantically calling us in the middle of the night. For some odd reason, as fate would have it, my phone didn't ring when they tried to reach me. Even though I had it by my bedside every night for six years, and I had handled endless emergencies in the night. That night, for whatever reason, thankfully, Kait picked up the call, immediately jumped in her car, and made it there just in time.

In those final hours, she lay beside him with her head on his chest. She told him it was okay to go. She told him how much she loved him, how much we all loved him, how proud we were to be his children. And she placed a small cross in his hand—the same cross that his own father had been holding when he passed many years ago, the one that had been kept all this time for this very moment.

My dad took his final breath being held by his one and only daughter, with his father's cross in his palm, and then the man himself—larger than life in every way that mattered—was gone.

I woke up bright and early only to see countless missed calls on my phone. Carin and I quickly headed over to the house. In no time, my phone rang again. It was the fire chief, who had already gotten word of my father's passing. He asked if he could come by with a few of the men to help escort Dad's body to the funeral home.

Within minutes, a call went out across the department. What arrived at our house was not a few men. It was a parade. Every rig they had, it seemed—fire trucks lining the street, thirty men in full gear standing at attention on our driveway, their hands at their sides, their faces solemn and steady. They came inside and took my father out slowly, with the kind of quiet reverence that only men who have served alongside someone truly understand. They loaded his body into the hearse, and then the whole caravan drove him to the funeral home in a procession that stopped traffic and turned heads all along the route.

I could barely contain myself. I had expected one or two of them to show up. When thirty appeared, the wave of love hit me so hard that the tears I had been holding back just came. There was no stopping them. And I didn't try.

The funeral director told me afterward that she had been doing her job for over thirty years. Never once, she said, had she ever seen someone brought to her with such a procession and such a spirit of reverence among the men who carried him. She said she knew right then that whoever had died must have been an extraordinary person.

She was right.

We held the funeral at St. Charles Chapel in Port Jefferson—the same church my father had brought us to hundreds of times over the years, the church where my family had grown up, where we'd sat in the same pews on countless Sunday mornings and holy days. Outside the church, the firemen stood at attention as the bagpipes played "Amazing Grace" and the morning light fell across their blue uniforms.

As we wheeled my father's casket slowly down the old church aisle, I turned and saw them. Not just the firemen from seven different departments who had come to honor one of their own. Not just the countless police officers who had shown up to assist. But there, filling the pews behind them, was my crew. My Celtic Quest family. Not only the longtime employees who had become my dearest friends over the years, but the younger deckhands, too, and the junior mates, and my office staff. They had all come. Every one of them.

My heart melted. As much as I was trying to hold it together, their love and support in that moment meant more than I could say. Two different families of service, standing shoulder to shoulder in the same church, honoring the same kind of loyalty. My father would have loved that.

During his services, I shared something I found while cleaning up my father's belongings. On his big wooden desk, among the papers and letters he had accumulated over a lifetime, was a copy of a letter he had typed out slowly with his big fingers and printed to include in a card to the family of one of his dearest friends from the firehouse—a man named John from the FDNY who had passed before him.

In the fire department, there are different types of trucks, including the ladder truck. Each person on the ladder truck has a specific task, one of which is called forcible entry—the job of taking tools and a sledgehammer to force open a locked door so the rest of the firemen can gain access to the fire. The men call it "forcing the door."

The final line of my father's letter to John's daughter read:

"Please know what an incredible man your father was. He was one of the best firefighters I ever met, and more importantly, he was my dear friend. I know he is in heaven now, at peace with God. I can only hope that when my turn comes and the Lord calls me home, that your dad will meet me at the gate to help me force the door."

From the church, the procession made its way through the village. Draped across Main Street near my boats was a huge American flag strung between two ladder trucks. Countless firemen and police lined the streets, saluting as we passed.

Then they turned and brought us to the top of Maple Place, the small hill overlooking the firehouse in Port Jefferson. There, too, yet another giant American flag had been draped across the road, and the firemen lined both sides, standing at attention in their dress blues, saluting as we passed. My father's name was printed on the sign outside the firehouse. The flag on the pole flew at half-mast.

They stopped the procession there, and in the stillness of that morning, the fire alarm sounded one final time. Over the radio came the words that every firefighter knows will one day be spoken for them:

Ex-Chief Desmond O'Sullivan has now answered his final call.

We then headed to the cemetery, where they played taps and fired the volleys and folded the flag and laid my father into the ground, next to my mother, for his final rest.

IN THE WEEKS THAT FOLLOWED, we all took a little time to decompress. The last few years had been such a roller coaster.

Sadly, there was one last piece that had to be settled. We had to sell the family home on Mount Sinai Harbor, which we all loved deeply.

My sister Kait stepped up and did something I know my parents would be so grateful for. Our family had filled that house with a lifetime of belongings—furniture, photographs, china, tools, books, all the accumulated treasures and trinkets of a family that had lived fully and loved deeply. Kait organized a free estate sale and, piece by piece, gave it all away to the community. Strangers and neighbors alike came from all over, and she handed each person a little piece of our family's history with a smile.

With great care, she chose just the right person for each item, especially my dad's rocking chair. I hope whoever is sitting in it now knows what a special seat it was, and what a good man it held for all those years. And whoever is sipping tea from one of my mom's prized teacups—the ones she picked up from her travels around the world—I hope they know they are sharing a cup that was once held by an angel.

On the final day of the closing, I drove slowly up the driveway one last time.

I was alone. It was a crisp fall day, and the golden sun beamed down across the sound, lighting up the place where we had been blessed to live for over five decades. It was autumn, and the leaves had started to turn their beautiful colors. A gentle northwest breeze flowed up off the Sound and up the rolling hill to our property, carrying with it the salt and the coolness of the water below.

I rolled down the window and looked out over my parents' land, down the path that led to the beach. And I could see it all. Every bit of it. The boy running down that hill with his fishing pole. The brothers casting off the rocks in the fading light. Our family gathered around the fire while mom brought out dinner, and someone started singing an Irish song as the whole house rang with laughter, music, and love. My humble beginnings on this harbor with the Celtic Quest. The beautiful wedding ceremony with Carin.

I thought of my parents. They had given me the courage to follow my heart. They had blessed me with the freedom to chase my passion and trust in the way I was called. Everything I had built, everything I had become, I owed to them.

What an honor it is to care for the people who gave so selflessly to you your whole life. What a privilege to love them through these past years.

I felt such gratitude for God and the army of angels who had carried me through all of this. For the winding road that sometimes looked like it was leading to a dead end, to failure, to ruin, but was actually curving toward something I could not see. A place where, in the end, it all seems to work out according to some plan far wiser than my own.

It was all there. Every moment. Every season. Every joy and heartbreak that had somehow added up to the most extraordinary life I could have ever imagined.

It was time to say goodbye to this chapter of life. And as much as my heart was heavy, what I felt more than anything—more than sadness, more than loss, more than the ache of knowing I might never walk down that path again—was a gratitude so deep and so wide that it filled me completely.

I heard my father's voice, reminding me of one of his favorite Irish blessings: "May the road rise to meet you, and the wind be at your back, and may the tide carry you safely home."

I wiped the tears from my eyes, looked to the sky above this magical place on earth, and said with all my heart:

"Thank you, God. Thank you for all the Giant Fish and Happiness."

Then I slowly rolled up the window and pulled up the driveway for the last time. The road home was quiet, and the autumn light filtered through the trees the whole way.

When I walked through the door, Carin was there, arms open wide, and our dogs came bounding over like they always do, tails wagging, full of joy. I held onto her for a long moment without saying a word. Then I took a breath. This was home now, and I was ready — more than I had ever been — for the next wondrous chapter of life.

Captain Des
April, 2026

Capt Des

Des with his brother John

The one and only Desmond O'Sullivan Sr, (AKA Big Des)

Big Des OSullivan fought fires into his mid 70's

Dad 88 years young

Des with his Dad on his favorite bench

My Magical Mom, Kathy O'Sullivan,
Always smiling :)

Des and Carin

Our dear sister Kait

View from our home overlooking
Mount Sinai Harbor. Where it all started.

Celtic Quest Fleet

Celtic Quest 2

Humble beginnings
on the CQ 1

Capt Chris Kadlec, Des and
Capt mark Dejong

Capt Mark with some of our great crew

ABOUT THE AUTHOR

Captain Desmond O'Sullivan will be the first to tell you he's just a regular guy from Long Island who happened to follow an unorthodox path.

Born and raised in Port Jefferson, New York, he grew up with salt water in his veins and parents who told him to chase whatever set his heart on fire. He chased it all the way through a Division 1 soccer career at Fordham University, through the long and unpredictable journey of building his own charter fishing company, the Celtic Quest Fleet, and into a life that taught him far more about faith, surrender, and gratitude than he ever expected to learn with a fishing rod in his hands.

When he's not fishing, Desmond is also a musician, composer, interfaith minister, and speaker who is passionate about helping others find purpose and peace in the middle of life's inevitable gales.

He wrote *Giant Fish and Happiness* not as an expert handing down advice, but as a fellow seeker sharing what the journey has shown him so far.

Desmond still owns and operates the Celtic Fleet in Port Jefferson, NY, which has been going strong since 2002.

He lives on Long Island with his wife, Carin, and their two dogs, Sunny Grace and Daisy Rose.

www.ingramcontent.com/pod-product-compliance
Lightning Source LLC
LaVergne TN
LVHW050623100826
845148LV00011B/1710

* 9 7 9 8 2 3 4 0 4 7 0 0 7 *